I0807340

Safe!

Chapter by chapter the crescendo builds of heart-wrenching stories of sexual assault against vulnerable children who are supposed to belong to the kingdom of heaven but are trapped in the dungeons of predators and wolves dressed in sheep's clothing. This book is a must read for everyone who cares about Jesus and his love for children.

—Rev Dr John Teke, Senior Pastor, Deputy Chairman of the National Ministers Fellowship of the Cameroon Baptist Convention

This book highlights the vulnerability of children and challenges us to be intentional and strategic in protecting them. Morrison, a father, grandfather, and pastor, brings his wealth of experience to the study on child safety and protection, urging us to care for these little angels that God blessed the world with. He exposes the complicity and complacency of the community and the church in how we have cared for children. Everyone who understands and appreciates children as the heritage of God needs to speak up for them and shield them from monsters who take advantage of their vulnerability. This piece focuses not on making excuses or casting blame but on taking action for the safety of the young, endangered generation. It offers a fresh perspective on how to care for our children. I highly recommend you read and apply it!

—Rev Dr Emmanuel O. Adewara, Pastor of First Baptist Church in Kubwa, Abuja, and Secretary of Pastors Conference of the FCT Baptist Conference, Nigeria

Well-researched, informative, and practical, this guide provides essential knowledge and tools to safeguard children from sexual abuse. Morrison breaks down complex concepts into understandable and actionable steps that anyone can follow. He covers risk management, policies and procedures, screening and selection, training, reporting and responding to abuse, and providing support to victims. We must create a culture of safety where everyone takes responsibility for protecting children and promoting healthy relationships. Real-life examples, case studies, and practical tips make this book relevant and applicable to a wide range of situations and settings. This much-needed resource fills a gap in the field of child protection. It is a valuable tool for anyone involved in the care and welfare of children.

—George Gumah, Child Safety Interviewer, Pioneers-Africa

As practical and indispensable as an umbrella in the rain, this book offers the church an invaluable tool against the lurking evil of child abuse. Careful biblical exploration of the value of children and the appropriate response to abuse cements the issue firmly in Scripture, leaving no room for doubt about the responsibility of believers in the matter. The author highlights the destructive consequences of abuse on the victim, guiding the reader in an appropriate, empathetic response. Morrison does not shy away from calling the church to stand for righteousness and justice in their dealings with the perpetrator. Complete with real-life stories, step-by-step guidelines, and relevant documentation, readers are equipped with everything they need to put measures in place to prevent child abuse and keep children safe.

—Lize Labuschagne, Lecturer at South African Theological Seminary

The story of Agnes being defiled by her father is one among a million similar stories happening in our society. Unfortunately, sexual abuse remains a weighty problem in our society, mostly a hidden crime. Most young people who are abused are groomed into trusting their abuser and are unlikely to realize that they are being abused. The abuser uses power imbalances in age, status, or physical strength to exploit children. The child may depend on their abuser and be too scared to tell anyone what's happening because they don't want to get them in trouble or risk losing them. Long-term consequences to sexual abuse include psychological, physical, and socioeconomic problems. Parents need to monitor their children at all times. This book provides a wide range of lessons and learned experiences for readers to benefit from.

—Rose Chemeli Rono, Living Room International Nursing Home (Kimbilio Hospice), Kenya

Safe!

How You Can Protect Children from Sexual Abuse

PHILIP E. MORRISON

OASIS INTERNATIONAL PUBLISHING

Safe! How You Can Protect Children from Sexual Abuse

Copyright © 2024 by Philip E. Morrison.
All rights reserved. Pages labelled as Resources may be photocopied for noncommercial use in an NGO or church setting. Otherwise, no part of this publication may be reproduced, distributed, or transmitted in any form or by any means, or stored in any database or retrieval system, without prior written permission from the publisher.

ISBN 13: 978-1-59452-876-7
ISBN: 1-59452-876-4

Published by Oasis International Ltd.

Oasis International is a ministry devoted to growing discipleship through publishing African voices.

- We ***engage*** Africa's most influential, most relevant, and best communicators for the sake of the gospel.
- We ***cultivate*** local and global partnerships in order to publish and distribute high-quality books and Bibles.
- We ***create*** contextual content that meets the specific needs of Africa, has the power to transform individuals and societies, and gives the church in Africa a global voice.

Oasis is: *Satisfying Africa's Thirst for God's Word.* For more information, go to oasisinternational.com.

The author and publisher have made every effort to ensure that the information in this book was correct at press time and disclaim any liability to any party for any loss, damage, or disruption caused by errors or omissions, whether such errors or omissions result from negligence, accident, or any other cause. However, if you feel that your work was not accurately cited, please reach out to us at info@oasisinternational.com and we will make every effort to review and correct the book where required. Furthermore, any internet addresses (websites, blogs, etc.), telephone numbers, or the like in this book are offered only as a resource. They are not intended in any way to be or imply an endorsement by Oasis, nor does Oasis vouch for this content.
Author contact information: philjanmorrison@gmail.com

Unless otherwise indicated, Scripture quotations are from the Holy Bible, New International Version® Anglicized, NIV® Copyright © 1979, 1984, 2011 by Biblica, Inc.™ Used by permission. All rights reserved worldwide.

Scripture quotations marked (KJV) are taken from the Holy Bible, King James Version, (Public Domain).

Scripture quotations marked NLT are taken from the *Holy Bible*, New Living Translation, copyright ©1996, 2004, 2007, 2015 by Tyndale House Foundation; Anglicized Text Version, © SPCK 2018. Used by permission of Tyndale House Publishers Inc., Carol Stream, Illinois 60188, USA, and SPCK, London, UK. All rights reserved.

Printed in India.

24 25 26 27 28 29 30 31 32 33 BPI 10 9 8 7 6 5 4 3 2 1

Dedication

This book is dedicated to all those who are involved in the nurture, care, teaching, and discipling of children in the churches of Africa. May God use you to promote child safety practices on behalf of the children he has entrusted into your care. Only eternity will reveal the importance of your ministry of protecting these little ones, for such is the kingdom of heaven.

"God is not unjust; he will not forget your work and the love you have shown him as you have helped his people and continue to help them" (Hebrews 6:10).

Dedication

Table of Contents

Acknowledgements

I am thankful for the incredible support of my wife, Jan, who has patiently affirmed my efforts and involvement in the area of child safety in my investigative role, my teaching opportunities, and the challenges that I face in my research and writing. I do not think I could function well in this ministry without her untiring and patient encouragement. Thanks also for your careful reading of the manuscript, your insightful comments, and "speaking for the common man" in helping to shape and simplify the writing.

I am very thankful to the former Presiding Bishop of the Africa Inland Church-Kenya (AIC-K), Dr Silas Yego, who readily gave his permission and affirmed this research within the denomination.

I am thankful for the illustrations, scenarios, practical applications, and suggestions, as well as encouragement and support provided by my colleague in child safety, Cath Swanson, Africa Inland Mission's Child Safety Officer. She is a wise and indefatigable champion for children both in the church in Africa and the mission community, and I have learned so much from her. She is a blessing to many. Her hidden work will not go unnoticed or unrewarded by Jesus!

I would like to acknowledge the help of many of my Kenyan pastor friends and former Moffat Bible College students who helped in the original research to arrange and facilitate the data-collection meetings in seven counties of Kenya. Their work in bringing the church leaders together to take the survey and in other ways was invaluable.

I am thankful for Dr Joy Mbaabu's cultural insights and illustrations, which helped to explain various issues about child sexual abuse within the African context.

I am very grateful for Hannah Rasmussen of Oasis, who has worked diligently and patiently with me to help transform the seminar version of this book to a more reader-friendly and helpful version. This was a difficult task because she had to immerse herself in the world of child sexual abuse, a world no one can deal with without experiencing some level of trauma. Yet she engaged in her work both empathetically and professionally and I am in her debt.

Thank you to Matthew Okeyo of the Africa Inland Church Child and Community Agency for Development, and Reverend Stephen Munyambu, and Rachel Kisyula from AIC Milimani, Nairobi, for their committee work in helping me to write and contextualize the Sample Policy Template, and Yohana Batano for his kind work of translating it into Kiswahili.

Finally, I want to thank my Lord and Saviour who highly valued children and modelled love and care for them when he "took the children in his arms, placed his hands on them and blessed them" (Mark 10:16). May I be like him!

Introduction

1
Unsafe?

When her father passed away, Sheila was devastated. She did not need anyone to tell her that his death signalled a bleak future for her. For instance, her hope of continuing with her education was now gone. A few months after her father's death, a paternal uncle came visiting. He offered to educate her, saying he would enrol her in a school in Nairobi. Sheila's mother gladly let her go. Sheila moved into her uncle's house on the outskirts of Nairobi and joined Form One at a day school.

For the first ten months everything was fine, but one evening her uncle invited himself into her bed, where he defiled her. She endured the abuse for months. Consequently, she became pregnant, and her uncle forced her to have an abortion and then resumed sexually abusing her. Again, she became pregnant and had a second abortion. However, this time she confided in a neighbour who reported the uncle to the police. She is now living in a shelter while her case drags on in court.[1]

Sheila's story is like that of many other children. This is because in many places child sexual abuse is commonly accepted, excused, or hidden. As we will see in this book, many boys and girls in Africa face child sexual abuse in various forms in their homes, communities, schools, and, sadly, in the churches and even in Christian Nongovernmental Organizations (NGOs).

Child sexual abuse in our society

Without question, the prevalence of child sexual abuse is alarming. A few statistics, using Kenya as an example,[2] illustrate the scope of the problem of the lack of safety for our children. According to Kenyan, Tanzanian, and international legal definitions a child is someone under the age of 18. One study found that in Tanzania nearly 3 in 10 (30%) females and approximately 1 in 7 males (14%) have experienced sexual violence prior to the age of 18,[3] similar rates to Kenyan levels of sexual violence in a 2010 study.[4] That would mean that in Kenya alone about 5.25 million children had experienced sexual violence, or more than the population of Nairobi![5] A 2019 Kenyan study found rates at about half this level: "Sexual violence was experienced by 15.6% of females and 6.4% of males before age 18 . . . Among females, 6.8% experienced unwanted sexual touching, 7.5% experienced unwanted attempted sex, 4.3% experienced pressured sex, and 4.3% experienced physically forced sex in childhood."[6] Either way, these percentages represent huge numbers of people. Not only that, but this number only represents a snapshot in time. Because the segment of the 18-years-and-under population changes from year to year, every year that means new specific children are becoming victims of child sexual abuse. Tragically, this means a substantial number of the population will deal with the physical and psychological ramifications of their abuse throughout their adult years.

We may find these numbers shocking, because child sexual abuse is often hidden beneath the surface. Often these practices are covered over or minimized as part of culture and thus rationalized, excused, and even accepted. Often these only come to light when some horrific act is committed, or a person of celebrity is involved. Adding to the child abuse that happens within the general society there is the commercial sexual exploitation and trafficking of children that often goes unchecked and unprosecuted. This lack of official action only adds to the acceptance of child abuse in society.

As we look at these numbers, we can see that many children in our communities are not safe and are at risk. Therefore, we must ask what we can do to provide protection and a safe environment for them.

Child sexual abuse in the church

We would hope that Christian organizations would be a safe place for our children. Serving as a missionary in Kenya from 1992 to 2019, I saw how God uses the church in amazing ways. My years of work in theological education introduced me to many leaders passionate about Scripture, mission, and living godly lives. In recent years, however, I have begun to see some of the hidden sins in our Christian community. After I received training in how to respond to reports of child sexual abuse with the Child Safety and Protection Network, I wondered what the presence of child sexual abuse might be in our churches.

This question became the subject of my doctoral dissertation, and I studied Child Safety within the Africa Inland Church, Kenya. Much of the material in this book comes from what I learned as I read on this topic and surveyed church members.

For the purposes of my research and this book, I used the World Health Organization definition of child sexual abuse:

> Child sexual abuse is the involvement of a child in sexual activity that he or she does not fully comprehend, is unable to give informed consent to, or for which the child is not developmentally prepared and cannot give consent, or that violate the laws or social taboos of society. Child sexual abuse is evidenced by this activity between a child and an adult or another child who by age or development is in a relationship of responsibility, trust or power, the activity being intended to gratify or satisfy the needs of the other person. This may include but is not limited to:
>
> - The inducement or coercion of a child to engage in any unlawful sexual activity.
> - The exploitative use of child in prostitution or other unlawful sexual practices.
> - The exploitative use of children in pornographic performances and materials.[7]

Because I worked with the Africa Inland Church of Kenya, I was given permission to research within that denomination. I conducted research in seven different counties in Kenya, in both rural and urban settings and in different tribal areas. After talking with colleagues in Tanzania and in other denominations, I am confident that the situation in many, if not most, countries and evangelical churches would be similar to what I found. So unless the AIC-K needs to be mentioned for clarity, I simply refer to "the church" in general throughout the book.

In my research I asked: "In your personal ministry, are you aware of any incidences of child sexual abuse within your local or other AIC churches?" In this broad representation of the population, 78 per cent (103 out 137 respondents) reported knowledge of child sexual abuse, and among them they were aware of 227 incidents of child sexual abuse. Thus, even in this small sample, we can see that child sexual abuse is a serious problem not only in our society or communities at large, but also, sadly, in our churches as well.

I asked about who the offender and the victim were:

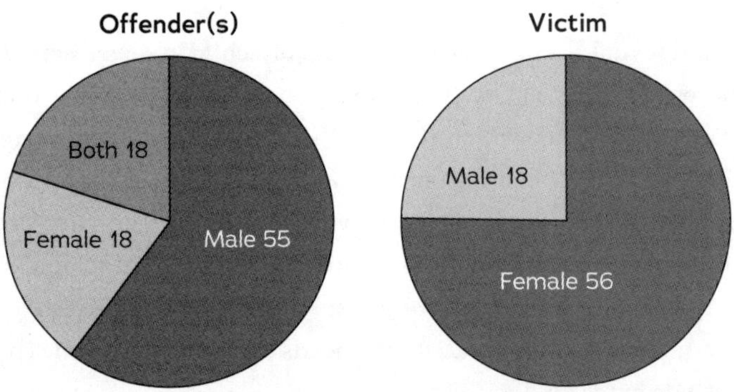

* Respondents could check more than one category for offender, but not for victim

Both men and women are abusing children, although respondents were twice as likely to know of male perpetrators (80%) as female perpetrators (40%). When it came to victims, both boys and girls are being abused, but respondents were three times more likely to know of cases where girls were victims.

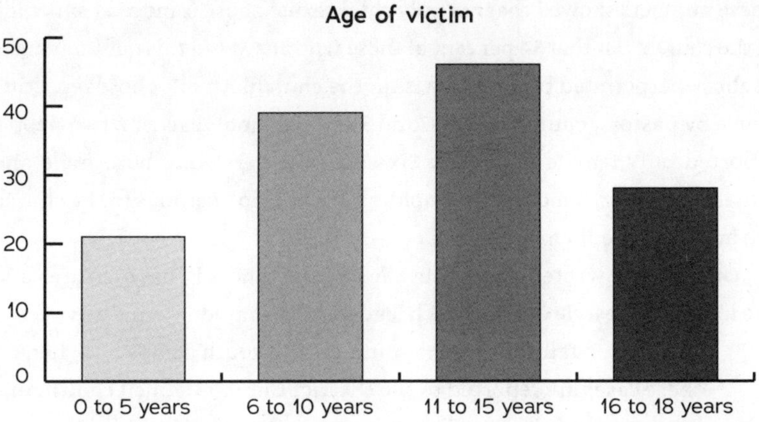

* Respondents could check more than one age category.

Unfortunately, children of all ages are being abused. While the numbers appear highest for the 11-15 age range, the 16-18 year range is also high given that it only represents a three-year span instead of a five-year span.

Although the numbers I uncovered are very sad, the situation in Kenyan churches is not unique. An American study by Calvin's Center for Social Research found that sexual abuse is often just as common within Christian circles as in the rest of society. Their study of abuse perpetrated by spiritual leaders within a congregation stated, "Studies and statistics today . . . indicate an incidence of abuse within the church equal to that in the general population."[8] Nor are Kenya or the US known for more child sexual abuse than other countries; statistics for child sexual abuse in the general population show similar levels around the world.

I wanted to find out whether the offenders were in church leadership:

The offender was:	
Pastor	21
Church leader	14
Sunday-school teacher	3
Other/none of the above	35

* (6 respondents knew of abuse by both a pastor and church leader. One knew of abuse by all three categories.)

These numbers showed that not only child sexual abuse is indeed happening in the church, but that 54 per cent of those who answered this question knew of abuse perpetrated by leaders within the church! Among those reporting abuse by pastors, church leaders, and Sunday school teachers, two people reported only female offenders. Six said offenders were both male and female. However, if most people holding leadership positions in the church are men, this would make sense.

One woman wrote to me about the circumstances in her own area and the immoral lifestyle of the church leaders. She shared:

- Pastors sexually harass the youth during youth camps . . . When these cases are reported to the District Church Council chairman, he dismisses it as a non-issue.
- They have extra-marital affairs with divorcees and other women. Some women [in] leadership realize this and tell these pastors that it is wrong. These pastors deny [any wrongdoing] . . .
- Some of them text girls to take selfies . . . while they are naked and send [the pictures] to the pastor.
- The preaching from these pastors [is] self-defensive and attacks those who discover their immoral lives.
- Whenever the elders are accused of immorality, the pastor cannot act or discipline because he is one of them.[9]

Her experience echoes what I found about the concerning level of child sexual abuse within our churches.

The other half of respondents said they knew of abuse by someone else who they encountered in their ministry. Perhaps the perpetrator was a member of the congregation or perhaps the victim was in their congregation but the perpetrator was an outsider. In the research survey, respondents were asked to write who these might be. One respondent wrote, "There are many children who are being abused in our country starting from our homes, i.e. being abused by their own fathers, others by their cousins and even others by the so-called family members . . . Again, others being abused by their neighbours, teachers, family friends and even others by strangers."[10] Since many of the respondents were themselves in ministry, their knowledge of abuse in the community reflects the reality that ministers are often called upon to help victims in times of crisis.

Child sexual abuse in NGOs

Perhaps you are not a church leader, but part of an organization that involves working with children. This may be a non-governmental organization (NGO), humanitarian agency, Christian organization, ministry of a church denomination, or an independent ministry. You might work with an orphanage, school, hospital, camp, feeding programme, or youth club. For the sake of clarity, we will use the term NGO for both NGOs and parachurch ministries and "church" for denominational and local congregational contexts.

NGOs mostly act outside of the church's sphere of influence and are independent entities subject internally to their boards and externally to governmental regulations of the country in which they operate. In terms of child safety, there needs to be strong internal structures and safeguards that will prevent child abuse, as well as procedures that deal transparently and decisively with any reported concerns of child abuse by their members.

Historically, there is ample evidence that there has been child sexual abuse perpetrated by NGO employees and volunteers simply because they often have easy access and opportunity to abuse children. The international charity, Oxfam GB, cited examples from three African countries in which 40 NGOs, both national and international, were implicated by name in that members of their staff were demanding sexual favours in return for goods or services.[11]

After citing these examples of abuse, they state in one of their training handbooks that:

> Uneven balances of power probably always exist between agency workers and beneficiaries. But in humanitarian situations the differential is extreme. Most beneficiaries (at least in the early stages of an emergency) are entirely dependent on agency workers for their very survival and that of their families. We have everything and they have nothing. It is easy for humanitarian workers to exploit this difference in power.[12]

In light of this, it is essential that the NGO, which is in the position of power, does everything to prevent the possibility of exploitation and to protect the children they serve.

In addition, the implementation of child safety measures by an NGO is important because those set out by governments may not be adequate. While the ideal would be robust governmental oversight of NGOs operating within their borders, this is not always the case. In *The African Report on Violence Against Children,* Maggie Black, speaking specifically of residential care NGOs as an example, writes:

> In Africa, evidence suggests that, in many instances, governments are challenged in their ability to provide effective coordination and oversight of alternative care measures, especially as residential care is largely provided by non-state organisations, which do not necessarily abide by the regulations and standards of the state.[13]

Although my research started within the church, I have realized that it is very relevant to leaders of NGOs as well. Therefore, throughout this book, if you are a Christian with influence in your church, NGO, or another organization that works with children, I will help you protect those under your care.

The church needs to address the issue

After the first data-collecting meeting for my doctoral research, a pastor came to me with tears in his eyes to tell me that his own daughter had been sexually abused. What was also sad was that he and his family were getting little support from the church, the community and especially from the police, but he said, "We are still pursuing." Unfortunately, his story and that of his daughter is not unique.

I asked in my research what was being done about the many incidents of sexual abuse those surveyed already knew about.

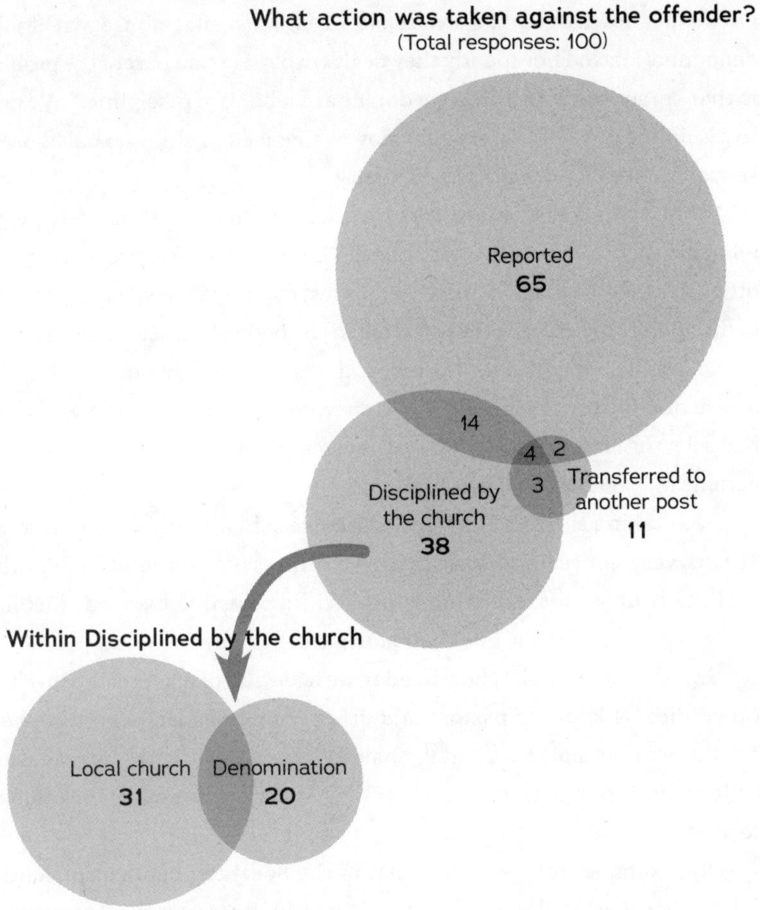

* Since 58 respondents were aware of multiple incidents of abuse, some of their responses may have reflected more than one incident.

Almost two-thirds (65) of respondents said the abuse was reported to governmental authorities. This is a good step. However, in some countries, people in church positions are required to report any child abuse to the government; by those standards this level of reporting is very low.

Slightly more than a third (38) of respondents said the church disciplined the perpetrator. Given the responses to the identity of the offender, it is possible that the victim was part of the church, but the perpetrator was not, so it would be difficult to exercise church discipline. However, some respondents clearly stated that church discipline was lacking. One Kenyan pastor acknowledged the existence of child sexual abuse within his denomination and how poorly they dealt with it. He said part of the problem is that "practically speaking we don't have a book of discipline." We need to discipline present leaders who may be involved in child sexual abuse or sexual immorality despite the difficulty.

While some perpetrators were transferred, there were very few people who said this was the only action taken. This is crucial, because perpetrators often continue their activity in other places; moving them without any form of discipline only spreads the infection in the body of Christ.

Of course, since these 103 respondents knew of 227 cases, someone aware of multiple cases could have answered based on all the ways they had seen the church respond overall, even if in each specific case the rate of actions may not have been as high.

Even taking that into account, 12 people said nothing was done at all! This is very concerning as it can give a message to the offenders that nothing is done to those who commit child sexual abuse and thus may encourage them to continue their abusive behaviour.

Unfortunately, in the church today we have a lot of what I call "Christian Cowardice." I know of pastors and other church leaders who have been caught in an immoral act and yet have not been dealt with. Instead, their colleagues hush it over, pretend it didn't happen, or just move the offender to another place.

One example from the US is that of the Southern Baptist Convention (SBC). For years the SBC leadership and its executive committee intentionally covered up sexual abuse in their denomination. However, in 2019 the *Houston Chronicle* brought the issue to light in three articles exposing sexual abuse and assault in the SBC, which forced them to set up an independent investigation to deal with the reports of the leadership's cover-ups over the years. This report describes what they found:

> For almost two decades, survivors of abuse . . . have been contacting the Southern Baptist Convention ("SBC") Executive Committee ("EC") to report child molesters and other abusers who were in the pulpit or employed as church staff. They made phone calls, mailed letters, sent emails, appeared at SBC and EC meetings, held rallies, and contacted

> the press . . . only to be met, time and time again, with resistance, stonewalling, and even outright hostility from some within the EC.[14]

When the church refuses to confront their leaders and members who are sexually abusing children, they are putting the value of their relationships over the value of dealing with evil and maintaining holiness in the church. They are acting like the Pharisees whom Jesus condemned in Mark 7:6-9 when they put their traditions above the commands of God. To minimize, excuse, or cover-up the grievous sin of child abuse is in clear violation of all that Scripture teaches regarding the church as a holy community and violates the commandment to "love our neighbour as ourselves."

Fortunately, since this report was made public, the SBC has accepted responsibility and taken steps to correct this situation. These include administrative oversight of long-term reforms, creating and maintaining an Offender Information system that is available to SBC churches, resources that include protocols, training, education, improving screening methods, and standard procedures for handling allegations of sexual abuse. Most importantly, the SBC has begun to acknowledge "those who have been affected by SBC clergy sexual abuse through both a sincere apology and a tangible gesture, and prioritizing the provision of compassionate care to survivors through providing dedicated survivor advocacy support and a survivor compensation fund."[15] This is a positive example of what can be done to address wrong actions from the past and to put into place measures to protect children in the future.

Satan doesn't want this evil in the church and in our society to be exposed. He wants to be able to continue the destruction of lives and ministries. That is why when we tackle child sexual abuse, we are engaging in spiritual warfare. Personally, as I researched the dark world of child sexual abuse, I found it extremely difficult spiritually. Therefore, as you begin this mission of making your church child safe, please be in much prayer as you and your fellow church workers go through the process.

The umbrella

One day I went out for a walk. As it was later in the day, I hadn't worn a hat. Since it was mostly blue skies, I didn't wear a jacket. Nor did I carry an umbrella. Suddenly, as one large white cloud wafted overhead, it started to rain! It was totally unexpected, and I was unprepared and unprotected.

In many ways, this is a parable of what can happen in a Christian community. Everything may seem fine. There is no sign of danger or trouble and then, suddenly and unexpectedly, the storm of child sexual abuse breaks upon us and we are unprepared to deal with it because we have not provided protection for ourselves.

We are living in a storm of sexual licence and permissiveness, of sexual violence and perversion, and we dare not ignore or deny it. Child sexual abuse is a problem not only in our society but, as we will see, in the church as well. One way to prepare and to protect our children, is for our churches and our NGOs to put into place a policy that will act as an umbrella to keep us dry in the storm. An umbrella is of no good if we don't use it, if we just leave it in the closet, if we don't open it up to provide protection.

The purpose of this small book is to help prepare Christian organizations, leaders, and their workers against the storm of child sexual abuse that threatens to engulf us. In my reading, the church's role in addressing child sexual abuse was hardly mentioned. Yet the church has resources and influence, so we could make a significant contribution in dealing with the scourge.

This guide will show you how to make our communities safer for our children. I acknowledge that this is a heavy subject. While I avoid unnecessary detail, due to the nature of the subject, a few case studies and biblical stories contain graphic language. In addition, we will explore biblical and cultural truths in order to lay a foundation for God's heart when it comes to the injustice that is child sexual abuse. I provide practical steps that show how to respond to child sexual abuse and care for victims. We will also explore ways you can prevent abuse and create a safe environment for children. I pray that this book will be the umbrella that we will take, open, and put in place over our organizations and ministries to keep our children safe.

PART I

The Value of Children

2

Cultural and Biblical Views of Children

The church must be involved in instruction about the value, worth and dignity of children from a biblical point of view. I believe that one of the reasons child sexual abuse hasn't been dealt with is because there hasn't been substantial instruction on the worth of children within our churches. This is important because, as we will see, the perpetrator's low view of the value and worth of a child is a factor leading to child sexual abuse.

However, before we look at the biblical view, we must look at trends in how African cultures view children. This is a generalization, since there are, of course, differences between various cultures in Africa.

Our ideals

Most cultures in Africa speak highly of the value and worth of children. For example, the *African Charter on the Rights and Welfare of the Child* states: "The child occupies a unique and privileged position in the African society."[16] In addition, it mentions "the inherent dignity of the child."[17] Commenting on the Charter, Thoko Kaime wrote, "[C]hildren are a valuable part of the society . . . [They] must be well protected and nurtured otherwise without them, society will die."[18] Thus, African traditional culture recognises the intrinsic worth of children and the need to protect them.

Many people and cultural practices in Africa highly value children. People sacrifice a lot to send their children to school. Parents take great pride in being known as the father or mother of their child. Special ceremonies celebrate a child's birth or naming. When a parent dies, a relative will often welcome the children into their home and raise them. Some people have even taken in children from the community after war or disease has left children orphaned. There are many other ways, too, in which our actions point to the fact that we truly value children.

Cultural risk factors

At the same time, we acknowledge that some aspects of cultural views do not express this value of children and put them at risk for abuse. We need to challenge these views and practices in order to fully value and protect children. In this section, I share insights from my friend Dr Joy Mbaabu on how some aspects of culture can be damaging and so contribute to the harm of a child. Dr Mbaabu is a lawyer, mediator, and transformational coach in Nairobi, Kenya. Unless otherwise noted, content in this section comes from her.

Traditionally, women's and girls' sexuality was owned by men. In some communities, men or boys had the right to "sexually play" with girls or women of their age, even when this amounted to sexual abuse or molestation. If reported, the woman or child would be laughed at for reporting what may be considered "normal" age-mate play. In some communities, it might have even been praised and elevated to something to be proud of, because it meant the woman or girl was attractive enough to arouse the man who sexually abused her. It is so heartbreaking when we consider sexual molestation normal in any way.

Closely related to this belief is the view that children are a man's property, which can have unintended consequences. When it comes to child sexual abuse, the National Director of the South African National Council for Child Welfare said that the "most fundamental [root problem] was how the children are being viewed: that children were a commodity."[19] Linda Richter adds, "Cultural values that encourage treating children as possessions pose no barrier to use of children to satisfy adult sexual desires."[20] Let's be clear: just because a culture may view children as a man's property does not mean that all men are or will be abusers. However, this view may prevent people from taking action when child sexual abuse is reported.

Viewing children as having less value and worth than adults can also open a door to abuse. Hassan O. Kaya reports that in South Africa, "Some men see children as inferior human beings who can be sexually abused at will . . . [M]en – regardless of racial and ethnic background – have so many privileges that they feel they have the right to do whatever they want, including sexually abusing children."[21]

Different groups of children also receive different treatment. The Tanzania Ministry of Community Development, Gender and Children's *Child Development Policy* states in Issue 57: "Due to different Tanzanian cultures and customs . . . boys are always preferred over girls, in schooling issues, they are always given the chance to play, rest and the right to recreation while girls are necessitated to help their mothers with domestic chores."[22] There could be economic reasons for this. Thoko Kaime gives examples of the choice parents had to make between their boy and girl children as to who would go to school because they had insufficient funds for school fees. But he concludes, "Whether the basis of the discriminatory act lies in the poverty of money or the poverty of mind, the very fact of it taking place reveals a belief that one particular child is worth less than another."[23]

More vulnerable still are children with disabilities, both boys and girls. *The African Report on Violence Against Children* states, "Half of the children with disabilities reported abuse at 1–3 times a week – this is more often than any other category of children."[24] It also says, "Girls with disabilities are . . . at higher risk of abuse and violence, which in turn can aggravate existing disabilities or create secondary disabilities such as psychosocial trauma."[25]

One of the facilitators at a child safety conference told of disabled girls in a children's home who were mute and couldn't walk or even move from their beds. Yet they were becoming pregnant and giving birth, because they were raped at will by staff members.

Children with albinism are the most vulnerable to abuse in some cultures. *The African Report on Violence Against Children* points this out:

> Children with albinism in Africa are sometimes seen as not fully human and may suffer severe discrimination. They are sometimes known as "children of the moon." In Tanzania, for example, people with albinism are referred to as . . . ghosts. In South Africa, albinos are commonly referred to as apes.[26]

Despite the high value of children and their rights laid out in the Charter, Charles Ohene-Amoh comments that this "does not protect the African child since child rights abuses such as defilement, corporal punishment, child trafficking, and child labour are on the ascendency throughout Africa."[27] Power and money can easily tempt people to violate children's rights. Unfortunately, sin means that no culture ever lives up to our ideals. For instance, Marcia J. Bunge wrote about European Christianity:

> The notion that children are fully human and made in the image of God has often been neglected in Christianity, and children have been referred to as "animals," "beasts," pre-rational," "pre-adults," "almost human," "not quite human," or "on their way to becoming human."[28]

As Christians, we also know that sin and the evil one prey on the vulnerable. We must thus stand against all forms of discrimination and remember that God identifies with the vulnerable. Jesus said that people who clothed the naked, fed the hungry, gave the thirsty something to drink, or visited prisoners were in fact doing it to him, and he could have said the same about people protecting vulnerable children.

The biblical view of children

Jesus's example and the Bible challenge all cultures by reminding us that children have value and worth because they are God's image bearers (Genesis 1:26).

Children are God's handiwork (Psalm 139:13-15), knit together or embroidered by God. They are "fearfully and wonderfully made", masterpieces of God's creation. In fact, speaking of humanity, which would include children, David writes: "You have made them a little lower than the angels and crowned them with glory and honour" (Psalm 8:5). Children are ranked a little lower than angels!

As we often say in Africa, children are a blessing from God. We see this in Psalm 127:3-5: "Children are a heritage from the Lord, offspring a reward from him . . . Blessed is the man whose quiver is full of them."

As we will explore in the next chapter, Jesus held a high view of a child's value and worth (Matthew 18:1-7). The seriousness with which Jesus views the harming of children and leading them astray demonstrates the value and worth he places on the child.

Finally, remember that children are people too! When we read in the Scriptures about how to treat each other with respect, kindness, and compassion, etc., God is not just talking about adults! He is referring to children too!

The value and worth of children must be taught not only from our pulpits but to the congregation at large and in other venues such as Sunday school, youth camps, Vacation Bible School, and in men's and women's fellowships as well. Teaching the biblical view of the value and worth of children will help change attitudes and the manner in which we treat our children. This will help us to build a culture of safety for our children.

We can also use our churches to raise awareness that child sexual abuse is real and affects us all. When a preacher talks about sexual immorality, he or she should not fail to mention child sexual abuse. When we are teaching children about how God protects us, let us help them to know how he uses us as safe adults to protect them. Do they know who is a safe person in the church? Who could they go to and tell if they were being harmed? Let us talk to boys about how they must respect their sisters and other girls.

As Christians, we must also address the culture's view of the value and worth of children where it falls short of biblical ideals. We must speak out like a prophet against evil or injustice against children, including sexual abuse. Our churches cannot remain silent on this issue. Wherever we see the harassment of the vulnerable we must reveal it and speak up. Break the silence!

3

Safe in the Arms of Jesus

Some women were meeting in Tanzania when the subject of child sexual abuse came up. Many of them expressed that it was simply expected that young girls would experience some type of sexual abuse. It was not a matter of "if", but "when." Obviously, their environment was not a safe place. This sad story points out the need for child safety in our society and in our churches. But what does a safe place look like and what should it be?

When a young child faces danger or distress, when they feel insecure, where do they instinctively go? They run to a safe place. A place that will shelter them from anything that threatens them. A place that will provide them with comfort and security. In this chapter we look at what a safe place would be like.

We see an example of this in Mark 10:13-16 in a story about Jesus, children, and those who did not see children as important. What was going on here? Parents were bringing their children to Jesus to have him touch them. But the disciples intercepted them and rebuked them as they clearly thought that children were not important enough to get to have time in Jesus's presence!

What was the cultural view of children back then? Children, along with women, old men, and slaves, were viewed as physically weak and considered burdens on society with little value in the wider life of the community. "In Greece and Rome, it was an accepted practice to abandon unwanted children along the roadsides to die."[29]

But the view of Jesus was different! The familiar New Testament picture of Jesus taking a child in his arms and receiving the child with love portrays an attitude of care and concern for children found nowhere else in the ancient world.[30] Jesus found time for children and often used them as illustrations of the type of people believers should be. He therefore rebuked the disciples for wanting to keep the children from him! He warned his followers not to despise children or to cause them to stumble. Children were valuable and were to be treated with love and care.[31] So, he took them on his lap. This was a safe place for them.

In this chapter we ask ourselves: How are our organizations taking care of our children? Are we more like the disciples or more like Jesus? We take care of what we value. What does the way in which we take care of children suggest about how much we value them?

How did Jesus care for children?

Jesus *protected* children. The disciples rebuked the children and their parents. They were obviously annoyed. They probably frightened and threatened the little ones as they tried to keep them away from Jesus. But Jesus protected them. No harm could come to those children seated in the lap of Jesus. No evil could harm them when they were safe in his arms.

Likewise, our congregations – representations of Christ's body – should be places of protection. Children today face much scarier threats than the disciples' rebuke, so we must intentionally and watchfully protect them from those who would seek to harm them. God has entrusted children into our care, so we should do everything in our power to put into action practical measures and polices that safeguard our children from the evil and devastation of child abuse.

Jesus *accepted* children. Jesus did not relegate children to second-class status. No, instead he said, in Matthew 19:14, "Let the little children *come* to me, and do not *hinder* them" (my emphasis). That is welcoming. That is acceptance. Do our churches welcome and accept children? That is what a safe place is all about. Acceptance speaks to our emotional needs. A welcoming place reassures us that we are loved.

When we treat them as children and not as adults, we accept children for who they are. We realize that they learn differently than adults and teach them in age-appropriate ways. For example, children love action songs and interactive teaching. We know, too, that little ones can't sit still for long, so we provide for their developmental needs and take into account their short attention spans. When we accept them as children, we recognise their needs in our churches.

Jesus *affirmed* children. Jesus continued in Matthew 19:14, "for the kingdom of heaven belongs to such as these." Jesus was ascribing great value and worth to the children. The disciples did not see them as being valuable or worthy enough to be in the presence of Jesus. They felt that only adults and the religious and society leaders had enough status to come to Jesus and occupy his time. But Jesus elevated the status of children and affirmed their value and worth.

We affirm children by encouraging them. Children, like all of us, thrive when they are given words of praise and encouragement – not just for achievements but for their effort. We can say things like, "You have tried so hard, I am proud of you!" These are words of life that build a child's self-esteem and confidence. Doing so won't make them conceited; rather, it will make them resilient and emotionally healthy.

Jesus also *blessed* children. Mark 10:16 says, "he took the children in his arms, put his hands on them and blessed them." A safe place is where children can receive the blessing of spiritual nurture, instruction, and encouragement.

We must also ask, "How do we bless our children? How do we affirm their value and worth?" In the church particularly, I think if we look at the budget, or the money spent on children's ministries, and compare that with what we spend on adult ministries we will be able to gauge whether we really affirm the value and worth of our children. So often, money is collected for a new keyboard or robes for the choir, yet there is never enough Sunday-school materials. We don't have to host fancy programmes, but simply use the resources we already have to provide quality ministries for children. We bless our children by investing time and resources in our children's ministries so that they receive spiritual nourishment.

From this incident in the life of Jesus, I believe the disciples learned an important lesson about children and how they should be treated. They saw that children were valued, accepted, affirmed, and blessed in the safest place on earth – the presence of Jesus.

PART II

Care for the Victim

4

Why Victims Don't Speak Up

We may say to ourselves, "If someone came to me and reported that they were being sexually abused, I would do something about it." This is good! However, it also suggests that we expect that our involvement and our responsibility begin only when we receive a report. We also probably assume that the victim will approach us and clearly explain what happened by providing full details.

However, for the victim, actually telling someone is often the *end* of a very long process. It can be very difficult to talk about and shocking and terrible to say out loud. How do you talk about something like that? The victim might not know who they are able to tell. And what will happen if they do say anything?

It is scary and risky for victims to speak up, so victims often watch for hints or indications that someone may be willing to listen before they decide to open up. Though we are not aware, our response to victims often begins before we even know that sexual abuse has taken place.

Sometimes a victim will test how someone is likely to respond by sharing only some of the information. Perhaps they say something negative about the perpetrator, or claim that this happened to someone they know. Victims do not usually approach the first person they talk to with a fully prepared, detailed report.

We, therefore, need to be aware that the first response a victim receives can have significant impact. If we respond poorly, we might lose the victim's trust and they might not share anything further with us. We might continue to believe that sexual abuse is not a problem in our organization, and yet it may be our response to victims that keeps them from speaking up.

The tragic tale of Tamar

The trauma of abuse is huge. Unfortunately, the way in which people respond – or fail to respond – can traumatize the victim even further. We see a terrible example in 2 Samuel 13, which tells us the horrific, painful, and violent story of Amnon raping his half-sister Tamar.

Amnon lusted after the beautiful Tamar. He, along with his friend, concocted a plan whereby he would be alone with her by pretending to be sick. When his father, King David, came to visit him, Amnon asked that Tamar make some food for him and feed him with her hands. David agreed. But when Tamar brought the food to Amnon, he overpowered her, raped her, and then forcibly threw her out of his house. Completely traumatized, she was taken in by her brother Absalom and stayed in his house. David was furious, but he did nothing. Two years later, Absalom had Amnon killed as an act of revenge – and conveniently got rid of his competitor to the throne.

While it may not have been *child* sexual abuse, it was nevertheless sexual assault and incest, resulting in tragic consequences. From this incident we can take numerous lessons to guide us about just how difficult it is for victims to speak up when they are abused.

Why is it difficult for victims to speak up?

POWER DYNAMICS

In Tamar's story, many people simply obeyed someone in charge. Amnon asked Tamar to make food for him and bring it to him. Her father, King David, told her to obey the request. Amnon told the servants to leave the room and they obeyed. Children obey their parents. Servants obey the prince. Younger sisters obey their brothers. Unfortunately, when someone is in a position where people are expected to respect or obey them, it is easy for them to abuse that power.

Dr Joy Mbaabu explains how children in many African societies are raised with the belief that adults are always right and are trained not to question or challenge an adult. Saying "no," to an adult is considered disrespectful and may have severe consequences, including being denied food or other basic necessities.

Of course, overall it is a positive value in African cultures that children are taught a healthy respect for their elders. They are taught to be obedient and serve them. I, Phil, am sad to see us losing this to some degree in the US, as it seems more children these days publicly disobey, talk back to, and even mock their parents.

However, respect for elders can also be taken too far. A teenage neighbour made inappropriate comments and tried to get a preschool girl alone so that he could touch her. One day he told the girl to fetch something from under the bed in his room. She obeyed. The boy followed her and shut the door behind him, trapping her in the dark bedroom, where he attempted to rape her.[32] It is thus important for children to know that they can refuse inappropriate requests, even if asked by an adult.

For girls, Kaime observes that, "Since respect is bandied about as an important aspect of virtue, submissiveness from the female folk is almost guaranteed."[33] In the worst-case scenarios, people in positions of seniority or leadership can abuse those under them by twisting the virtue of respect into a demand for compliance and thus sexually take advantage of younger people. There is thus potential for abuse wherever there is a power differential, and we know that globally women and children have less power than men.

The social status of elders can also prevent a child from reporting an incident. They may fear being told they are being disrespectful or not even being believed. Dr Mbaabu explains that when a child who has been sexually violated reports the incident to an adult, she or he might be rebuked by being asked something like, "Are you in your right mind? Your father, uncle, pastor, etc. cannot lie. He is an elder." It is assumed that it is the child who is lying. When it comes to the church context, positive religious beliefs such as respect and protection for the child are masked by strong cultural practices such as patriarchy and eldership, and thus there is often silence or passive treatment of child sexual abuse in the church.

Obedience or respect should never come before someone's safety. As we discuss in a later chapter, as Christians we are called to advocate for the oppressed. As adults and leaders, we need to use our social status and power to protect children and other vulnerable groups.

THREATS OR INTIMIDATION

It is common for perpetrators to threaten children in order to get them to comply with sexual demands. In Tamar's story, we are told that "since he was stronger than she, he raped her" (2 Samuel 13:14). Men are often stronger than women, and adults are bigger and stronger than children, so they are able to hurt the child if the child does not comply. Sometimes a perpetrator will use a weapon such as a knife or gun to threaten the child.

Even a verbal threat of violence can be very intimidating. Perpetrators often tell children, "If you ever tell anyone about this, you will regret it." They may even threaten to hurt or kill the child or the child's loved ones. Is it any wonder that a child will have difficulty reporting an incident to the authorities?

Children need to know that they will be safe if they tell. We see that when Tamar told Absalom about the rape, he provided Tamar with a safe place to live in his own house. We need to send a clear message: "If anyone ever makes you afraid or says they will hurt you or your family, tell a trusted adult. It doesn't matter if they told you to keep a secret or said they would hurt you if you told. If you tell me, I will keep you safe."

SEXUALITY IS TABOO

Absalom told Tamar to be quiet, not to talk about it. David appears not to have talked about it either. David fasted and mourned for Bathsheba's son when he was sick and dying and his advisers saw his grief. David wrote a lament for his friend Jonathan and even his enemy, Saul, when they died. But when his own daughter was raped, he was strikingly silent. Apparently, this was not something to be grieved or talked about.

Sexuality is a taboo subject in most African cultures. Many parents do not talk about sexuality with their children because they are afraid that talking about it will cause children to become sexually active. Friends have shared that their mothers warned them, "Don't touch boys! If you touch a boy you will get pregnant!"

As you can imagine, this tends to cause confusion for children. Suppose a man tells a young girl to touch him in a sexual way. Now the girl may feel shame because she feels that she has disobeyed her parents' warnings to never touch a boy. She may believe that she is at fault and be afraid of being punished if she reports the incident.

Suppose an adult exposes themselves to a child, takes a photo of the child undressed, or shows a child pornography. None of these involve "touching a boy", yet they are still sexual abuse. The child might feel uncomfortable and afraid, but they don't know how to talk about what has happened to them.

Because talking about sex is taboo, Dr Mbaabu explains that children who are abused have no way or no forum of reporting the incidents. If a boy or girl begins to narrate it, they may be shamed and asked to abstain from such "obscenity".

While information about sexuality should indeed be age-appropriate, children need to be able to talk about sexuality in order to report abuse. If children know the names of their body parts, they will have the vocabulary to explain what happened to them. They need to be told what boundaries cannot be crossed. They also need to be told that if anyone ever crosses those boundaries, the right thing to do is to tell their parents or another trusted adult. We will talk about how to create a safe environment for children to speak up in Chapter 11

SECRECY

When children are sexually abused, the perpetrator often warns them, "Do not tell anyone. This is our little secret." For the child to share what happened, they often need to have someone else tell them they should never keep such actions secret and that they should speak about it to someone they trust.

However, even if a child tells someone, their report of sexual abuse may not actually come to light because of a culture of secrecy to protect the family. As we can see in the story of Tamar, Absalom told her, "Be quiet . . .

He is your brother." In other words, "It is simply in our family, so don't let it worry you." As if that would make it right!

Dr Mbaabu mentions a Meru proverb that says, "*Mantu ja nja i janja*," which loosely translated means "Issues of the family belong only to the family." So this is the response a child gets when she reports the incident to another person, possibly even an elder. The aim here is to cover the family's shame and guilt, and manipulate the child to prevent them from telling the truth.

Thus, a child will easily keep secret what has been done to them, including sexual abuse or molestation. Being encouraged to hide the sexual violence can cause further trauma because the child is forced to participate in keeping the secret. It is as if the perpetrator's words, "It's our little secret" are being repeated – but this time by someone the child trusted enough to confide in.

When a victim tells us what happened to them, we shouldn't *force* them to report the matter to the authorities. We may, however, offer to speak on their behalf, or accompany them. If the child is a minor, however, we may well need to report it on their behalf. In some countries, there are laws requiring mandatory reporting to authorities if a minor (typically under the age of 18) discloses abuse. For adults, we can encourage them to tell the relevant authorities, but should not report on their behalf. How to report abuse is the topic of Chapter 7.

BELIEF THAT THEY ARE AT FAULT

Victims often struggle to tell people about abuse because they feel that in some way it is their fault or that they could have prevented it. Christians teach that sexual activity outside of marriage is sinful, dirty, and shameful, so children often have the same associations with their own sexuality. So, when someone is violated, it is easy for them to believe that they are now dirty or sinful. The feelings of shame can be very intense. But the victim did not sin! They are innocent, suffering because of someone else's sin.

People often give advice, especially to girls and women, about how they should act in order to avoid being viewed sexually or how they can avoid unsafe situations. For instance: Don't dress like that. Don't go there.

Don't walk alone. Carry something to protect yourself. Scream, run, or fight back.

When a victim is abused, they might remember all that advice and think, "I should have done ___" or "If only I hadn't done ___." In some way, they may believe that what happened to them is their fault or that they could not protect themselves. Sometimes people may even make insensitive comments, such as, "What were you wearing? Why were you out at night?" No one ever deserves to be molested or violated. It does not matter what they wear, do, or say. There is never a valid excuse to sexually abuse someone else.

What is more, a perpetrator is more powerful than the victim. Just like Amnon, they have planned and decided to take advantage of the victim. They are often able to do what they want no matter what the victim does, so a victim cannot expect to have been able to prevent the abuse. Neither can we expect a victim to have escaped, protected themselves, or cried for help. This is true for any victim, but especially children!

Of course, when something unthinkably bad happens, it is normal for us to want to try to find a reason. Sometimes, blaming yourself seems to give you some control over the situation. The rationale is that if something bad happened because you did something, then you can control the situation by avoiding doing that thing again. But typically the only way to prevent abuse from happening again is to bring the perpetrator to justice.

When a victim shares what happened, do not ask questions such as, "What were you doing? Didn't you suspect something was wrong?" It is very important that we tell victims, "This is in no way your fault. No one deserves to be abused. You did nothing wrong. The perpetrator sinned against you."

FEAR OF STIGMA OR PUNISHMENT

Even though neither molestation nor sexual abuse is the victim's fault, the shame can indeed damage the victim's reputation. Tamar asked Amnon, "Where could I get rid of my disgrace?" This cry of an anguished heart focuses us on the fact that the victim will not only struggle with the physical violation, but also with the emotional and spiritual violation, which will affect her or him for many years.

After the incident, Tamar tore her robe and put ashes on her head and went away crying. We read about the end result for Tamar in 2 Samuel 13:20, "And Tamar lived . . . a desolate woman." In other words, she lived in her brother's house and never married. However, perhaps because Tamar never had children, Absalom named his daughter after her. The shame affected her future, but it was not the end of her story.

The shame and stigma that comes with abuse can be very difficult for a victim. A girl who had just turned 14 was raped while fetching water. It soon became known throughout the village and she no longer wanted to go to school, because all the children knew of the rape and teased her. In addition, people were inevitably curious and there was the possibility of misinformation and gossip being spread.

A victim might be afraid to speak up because of how people might see them. So when we hear about sexual abuse, confidentiality is essential. Of course, reports may need to be made to the authorities and individuals who are able to provide care may need to know. Much of the detail does not need to be repeated, however. We need to shelter the victims from public ridicule and shame. We do this by keeping the identities of the abused and details of the abuse as private as possible.

The difference between confidentiality and secrecy is who is being protected. Secrecy protects the perpetrator. It also protects the institution's reputation – the church or the NGO. Secrecy prevents justice and care for the victim. Confidentiality, on the other hand, protects the victim. It discloses only information that would bring the victim care or justice, or information that would prevent further harm to others. It conceals information that would bring the victim further shame or pain.

NO ONE WILL LISTEN

After the rape, Absalom, Tamar's brother, asked her, "Has that Amnon, your brother, been with you?" (2 Samuel 13:20). Undoubtedly, he knew what had happened, but he did not seem to be concerned for Tamar's welfare. Absalom then belittled what happened by implying the rape was not that bad, as he says, "Don't take this thing to heart." Tamar knows she is disgraced! How could she not take her violation to heart? But Absalom says it is not that big of a thing. This is an example of inconceivable insensitivity and yet it is often what many victims experience.

One girl told her mother that their neighbour had touched her inappropriately. Her mother, who was ironing clothes, never even looked at her, but simply said, "Don't say that. He's a nice man."

Sometimes when a victim tells what happened, the other person does not believe them. Of course, sexual abuse is shocking. It is difficult to believe that it could happen to someone you know – or that someone you know could actually do that to someone else. You may not want to believe that your church leader or your employee or relative did such a thing. But we should never express disbelief or question the victim. Don't say, "Seriously? How can that be true? No way! That person would never do such a thing. Are you sure? Is that really what happened? We don't want to spread rumours or make false accusations."

It has already taken a huge amount of courage for the victim to share this traumatic experience. Such statements imply that you doubt that the victim is telling the truth – or worse, that you think they are falsely accusing someone. Unfortunately, this response is too common and as such becomes even more traumatic for the victim.

Jennifer Greenberg shares from her experience the importance of having her story being taken seriously:

> Even well-intentioned people sometimes don't know how to respond when we say we've been abused. I once confided in a church friend who stopped me, saying, "Let's not talk about that. That's what we have pastors for." All I wanted was for her to listen. All I wanted was for someone to be with me, to act as though it mattered – as though I mattered.[34]

Instead, the victim needs you to listen. They need to hear you say, "That is terrible. I am so sorry this happened to you. Thank you for trusting me with your story. I believe you."

IT WON'T MAKE A DIFFERENCE ANYWAY

When Amnon began to assault Tamar, she said, "What about me?" This is the distraught question of the victim. Tamar was old enough to know and understand what was about to happen to her. Younger victims of sexual violence and abuse may not know or understand what is happening in that moment, but the time will come when they raise the same question as they try to come to grips with their violation. Amnon ignored Tamar. Perpetrators do not care what happens to the victim. They care only about consequences to themselves.

So Tamar tried appealing to his self-interest, "What about you? You would be like one of the wicked fools in Israel." But Amnon ignored her. He was a prince, after all. Perpetrators often believe they will get away with it, especially if they enjoy high status in the community.

For a while, Amnon was right. Nothing happened to him. See 2 Samuel 13:21: "When King David heard all this, he was furious." But still he did nothing! The king's inaction was a further injustice against Tamar, and yet this is what so often happens.

Tamar's first question focuses our concern on the victim's welfare and healing. This should always be our priority. But too often there is more concern for the perpetrator than for the victim. Even after Amnon was murdered, there was more grief expressed for him than for Tamar. As the other sons of King David returned to the palace, 2 Samuel 13:36 tells us that they were "wailing loudly" and "the king, too, and all his attendants wept very bitterly." But, sadly, we see no such response to Tamar's rape.

Later, Absalom took matters into his own hands and killed Amnon in revenge. But he had selfish motives for that too: Amnon was the first in line to the throne. Was Absalom's concern for the victim really his focus?

The welfare of the victim should be our primary concern, but like Amnon, David, and Absalom, we often care more about our own agendas or reputations.

For instance, Dr Joy Mbaabu says that if a child who has been abused tries to report the incident, she typically speaks first to the mother. The mother tends to remain silent about it, partly to protect the male offender and family, and partly out of fear of backlash from others in the community if she takes the matter any further. She fears she will be blamed because she is the custodian of the child, and so the sexual violation must have been a failure on her part. Sometimes, if the father is the abuser, the mother will try to keep it quiet because he is the family breadwinner, and she and the children will be left destitute if he is convicted and imprisoned.

Many church leaders want the abuse to remain hidden in order to protect the reputation of both the church and the perpetrator – especially if the perpetrator is a leader in the congregation. David's response is like that of many church leaders. I wonder if part of the reason David did nothing was because he felt it was partially his fault. He had ordered Tamar to go into the room and feed her brother. Perhaps he did not discipline Amnon because he had done something very similar. David had abused his power to take Bathsheba to his palace, though she was not his wife, and sleep with her. When she became pregnant, he had covered up his sin by orchestrating her husband Uriah's murder.

Reflecting on David, I wonder if the reason we do not act when it comes to sexual abuse is because of the sin in our own lives. We must be people of spiritual and moral integrity to confront sexual sin. What that means is that we must be willing for other people to hold us accountable. We must not abuse our power to take advantage of people weaker than we are. And when we do, we must confess and repent of our sin. This will give us the authority and the credibility that we need to confront sexual abuse in our churches.

When victims see people who prioritize child safety and confront sexual abuse, they gain confidence and motivation to speak up. If your church or NGO creates a child safety policy, victims will realize that they are important. If another situation of abuse comes up in conversation and the leadership talks compassionately, victims are more likely to think their story will be heard and taken seriously. If leaders in your community express through their words or their actions that they will hold offenders accountable, victims have hope that by speaking up they can prevent others from being abused.

Listen first and watch for signs

My friend who worked in a children's home said, "We must also equip our girls to have a voice. Girls do not feel safe within the culture to speak up." Given all that we have just described, I want to paint a picture of how the child who has been sexually abused is feeling and why someone would not feel safe to speak up.

They are often afraid that if they speak up, the perpetrator will hurt them or their loved ones. But if they don't speak up, will the perpetrator not simply continue to hurt them or others? Will their speaking up make a difference? Or will they simply be labelled and isolated? They may feel betrayed and angry. Their safety, their bodies, their privacy has been violated. Someone they knew – an adult who was supposed to protect them – broke their trust. Can they really trust anyone again? They feel grief at what they have lost. They feel alone. Will people listen to them, or will they simply dismiss them – or even worse, blame them for what happened?

If you wondered at first why people don't speak up, you may now be wondering how anyone gets the courage to speak up at all!

Sometimes children may not actually verbalize that they have been abused. Instead, they may show physical signs that suggest that they have been abused. As a parent or a leader, learn to recognize warning signs that a child may have been sexually abused or that an adult, adolescent, or another child may be touching your child in a sexual way.

Here are some examples of possible signs and symptoms of abuse:

- unusual tearfulness,
- changes in mood,
- behavioural problems,
- resistance to see a certain person,
- bed wetting,
- sexual play,
- sexualized speech above their age level,
- irrational fears,
- a drop in performance at school,
- nightmares,
- and anger.

We should note that the existence of these signs does not automatically mean that the child is being sexually abused. However, if they are accompanied by other concerns, we need to look carefully and quickly into what is happening in the child's life and experience.

Sometimes children may bring up an incident indirectly. They might not be very clear, just dropping a hint or saying something vague. Perhaps they don't have the language to express themselves. Maybe even naming the act aloud is too terrifying for them. Perhaps they are afraid of how others will respond so they are testing what that response may be first.

Some adults, too, are reluctant to share the details of child sexual abuse – whether it was something that happened to them as children or suspected abuse of others that they are trying to report. This is a shameful topic that is taboo in some cultures. People may be afraid that by bringing it up they will bring shame on the family or community. Other reasons may be that they do not have the full details of the incident or are afraid of retaliation from those who have committed the abuse. However, their report should still be taken seriously rather than being dismissed for lack of evidence.

This is why whenever we hear even a hint of sexually inappropriate conduct, we must be very gentle and patient, listening to the person disclosing the abuse and helping them to feel safe. This can help them gain confidence to open up.

Leslie Vernick, who is a licensed clinical social worker, writes,

> Here you need to be very cautious. Listen hard, talk little . . . Studies show that abuse is traumatic but disclosing abuse can be more traumatic when the victim isn't believed or [is] blamed by those trusted to help.
>
> You represent God to the victim who asks for your help and justice. *Does God care about what happened to me?*
>
> I know that you want to represent Him well. And the best place to start is with compassion and care so that the victim feels heard, believed, and loved (emphasis hers).[35]

Yes, God cares about what happened to victims. Let's return to the story of Tamar for a moment. Although it is a tragic tale, my editor Hannah

Rasmussen points out a comforting fact that we often overlook: There was no one else was in the room when Amnon raped Tamar, yet somehow we have the story from Tamar's perspective, recorded in 2 Samuel for generations. What that means is that Tamar's family did not, in fact, succeed in keeping her quiet.

Despite all the men who betrayed her, Tamar still spoke out. She spoke out even as she was being raped. Tamar had been overpowered by someone stronger – someone who was next in line to the throne. She told Amnon what he was doing was wrong. She confronted him with the consequences of his actions. After it happened, she did not keep it as "their little secret", even though that came at a great cost to her. She publicly voiced her lament and shamed Amnon for his crime.

What courage it must have taken her to speak out!

Not only did Tamar speak out – someone listened. Someone took the time to listen to her story, and record her story, and publicize it to the whole nation. Someone believed her. Someone spoke up for her and told the truth. Whoever wrote 2 Samuel thus held Amnon and Absalom and David accountable for their actions for posterity.

In fact, we see that Amnon, Absalom, and David all experienced painful consequences for how they acted later. God himself saw what had happened to her and acted to bring about justice. Victims need to know that God saw, God cared, and God acted. God has not forgotten their plight. The way we respond can show the victim that God cares.

5

Provide Resources for the Victim

Knowing how difficult it is for victims to speak up, we realize that often we must speak up on their behalf. Children especially have no power to speak in their own interests. Proverbs 31:8-9 says, "Speak up for those who cannot speak for themselves, for the rights of all who are destitute. Speak up and judge fairly; defend the rights of the poor and needy." If someone confides in you about abuse, you might not have the authority to discipline the perpetrator, but you do have the ability to advocate for the victim.

In my survey of Kenyan AIC members, I asked those who mentioned that they were aware of child sexual abuse to share what the church had done to help the victim.

What help was given by the church to the victim and victim's family? (Total responses: 103)

Type of Action	Yes	Only this help given
Medical examination and treatment for victim	52	10
Counselling for victim	68	9
Counselling for the family	52	1
Legal	24	0
Financial	22	2
Nothing	11	
Unknown	2	

About two-thirds saw the church provide counselling for the victim, and half said the church counselled the family. Often this was pastoral counselling rather than trauma therapy. Half also said the church helped with medical support. There were cases where the church did nothing (10 per cent) or gave only one type of help (21 per cent), but often respondents witnessed more than one form of support. Since many respondents indicated knowing about multiple cases, it is possible that these multiple forms of support referred to various cases rather than multiple forms of support on a specific case.

Ideally, the church would offer as many forms of support as the victim needs. This chapter will give you ideas about the various types of support you and your church can offer to victims. These are practical steps we can take immediately, separate from questions of discipline and justice regarding the perpetrator.

Physical safety and health

The first action is to shelter victims from further abuse. This is done by providing them with a safe place away from the perpetrator in order to prevent further traumatization. The continued presence of the perpetrator would cause further trauma for the victim. Typically, putting distance between the perpetrator and the victim should be accomplished with minimal disruption to the child's life. For instance, the perpetrator would need to step down from their position and be barred from access to places where they may come in contact with the victim, such as the compound or premises of the organization, church, or school. In some cases, the victim may have to be moved to a safe location. For instance, if sexual abuse was taking place within the home, have the victim stay with a trusted family member or neighbour.

In cases where there is a possibility that penetration might have taken place, it is important to immediately provide medical examination and treatment by a doctor. This is important for the health of the victim. If the child has been raped, certain physical evidence is also required to prove the matter in court. This process must be carried out by a compassionate professional and in a timely manner. Of course, penetration does not have to take place for behaviour to qualify as sexual abuse. Sexual abuse can include fondling, taking pictures, exposure to pornography, or lewd conversation.

Listening

In addition, the church needs to provide pastoral care to the victim and the victim's family. We can provide this care by the gift of our presence. When they are ready, we can encourage them to tell their story and quietly listen to them as they express feelings of anger, shame, loss, and emotional pain. As Jamie Ivey counsels, "Many times, religiosity urges us to try to get the correct answer for their problem, grief, or trial. The first thing we can do as friends is offer our presence before we offer our answers."[36]

Many who have been abused have found that being able to tell their story and being believed has been a significant help in their journey toward healing. Sometimes this will happen some time after the abuse has taken place. I once sat with a man who had been abused more than 50 years ago. He told me and my colleague things he had never shared with anyone else before, including his wife. When he was finished, there was an amazing change in his countenance and demeanour. He felt deep relief. A burden had been lifted, simply because we believed him and validated his experience. Since then, he has gone for counselling and therapy and has begun to experience healing.

Listening should be done sensitively by coming alongside with prayer, scripture, and comfort. What has happened to the victim is traumatizing enough, but that trauma can be made worse by the way people respond to it. Don't downplay what happened by quoting verses such as "in all things God works for the good of those who love him" (Romans 8:28). When we try to focus on the good in a situation that is so evil, it can appear as though we are minimizing the pain the victim has experienced. Refer to the previous chapter for more advice about how to respond to victims, and in the next chapter we will go into more detail about spiritual encouragement for the victim.

Counselling

Along with pastoral care, the church should help the victim get counselling. The traumatization that results from sexual abuse is deep and long lasting, as seen with the man I mentioned above going to therapy 50 years later. I have looked into the eyes of children who have been molested and wondered what their future will be like as they deal with their trauma on an ongoing basis. When child sexual abuse happens, it is like throwing a hand grenade into the midst of a family, a church, a ministry. The damage and trauma are long lasting, and most victims will need ongoing counselling and therapy to help them be restored spiritually and emotionally.

When we think about the fact that in Kenya one out of six girls and one out of sixteen boys say they experienced sexual abuse, we realize that a substantial part of the population will be dealing with the physical and psychological ramifications of their abuse throughout their adult years.[37] There is a great need and opportunity for the church to be involved in providing counselling and healing ministry.

If at all possible, look for someone who is trained as a professional counsellor rather than taking this on within your organization. Professional counsellors are trained in how to address trauma, and the child may feel safer talking to someone outside the organization where the abuse happened. Your church or organization could draw up a list of such people as a resource for victims. If your church has a benevolence fund for people in need, you could use that to cover the cost.

Providing help to victims early can reduce the effects and speed up their healing. Wendy Maltz, a psychotherapist and author on sexual healing, gives hope for the victim long-term and into adulthood when she writes,

> Survivors can recover from the effects of sexual abuse using steps that involve recognizing effects, dealing with memories, overcoming guilt feelings, developing self-trust, grieving for loss, expressing anger, disclosing the abuse, resolving feelings toward the offender, improving health care, and learning that sex can be safe, healthy, and enjoyable [in marriage].[38]

Legal support

Additionally, the church should seek to help the victims of abuse when it comes to the legal process. To be a helpful resource for victims, find out about your country's laws regarding child sexual abuse, what a child's legal rights are, and what legal protections are provided. Learn about the child protection agencies in your area. Make a list of resources you can call for advice, information, and help. Include the phone numbers and email addresses. Parents can also do this to create a child safety plan for protecting their children.

Often, for healing to be complete, justice must be pursued and accomplished. Determine whether involving the local police and civil authorities would be helpful for the child, or if bringing them into the situation would cause further harm and trauma. I was told that in one country, parents would never involve the local police because, "It would be hell for the child."

Unfortunately, law enforcement officials do not always take abuse seriously or handle reports competently. In addition, court systems are notoriously slow, which means that cases may drag on for years, making the whole process financially impossible to resolve. This is where the church can step in to help support the process, both with their encouragement to persevere and their financial provision. If it is determined that the child would suffer more harm if the authorities were involved, it would be better to seek private medical help and counselling rather than retraumatize the child. We will discuss this more in Part III.

Be a supportive community

Providing a positive example and safe environment is an important way that the church can help survivors heal. Diane Langberg summarises this vital role in the victim's life as the church intentionally connects with survivor when she writes:

> Since many survivors have never seen healthy male-female relationships or family interactions these connections have inestimable value. It is wonderful for them to observe men and women treating each other with love and respect, asking forgiveness and seeking restoration, nurturing children in loving and safe ways, using touch appropriately in relationships, and above all, actually living out in relationship what God has called us to. The church community, if it will heed the call, has the privilege of providing the survivor with the family and friendships she never had.[39]

As the church is involved in caring for the abused, the body of Christ can come alongside those who have often lost or have very little support as they deal with the trauma of abuse.

Conclusion

We must speak up for victims to obtain the help and assistance they need as a result of the abuse. This means speaking to the police and government agencies, especially because as children, victims are unable to address these officials. This means insisting that they receive medical help and trauma counselling. In addition, we must speak on their behalf in matters of justice and where the church needs to deal with the perpetrator as a matter of discipline, because it would be difficult, if not impossible for victims to speak for themselves.

6

Spiritual Encouragement for the Victim

What comfort can be given to victims of abuse? What biblical hope is there for holistic healing and restoration for those who have suffered child sexual abuse?

How could God let this happen to me?

When something terrible happens, we often ask God why. Job is famous in the Bible for suffering. His health, children, and wealth were all taken from him. He questioned God, asking what he had done to deserve this treatment. His friends tried to tell him that bad things only happen to bad people, so if he was suffering he must have done something to deserve punishment. But at the end of the book, God revealed himself and said the accusing friends were mistaken. What no one knew was that, up in heaven, Job had actually been chosen because he had done nothing wrong. This was an attack by Satan, not a punishment from God.

Perhaps you can identify with Job. Something unthinkably terrible may have happened, but that does not mean that God is punishing you. It does not mean you did anything wrong.

For Christian leaders, we need to be careful not to fall into the trap of Job's friends, explaining why all this terrible suffering is God's intention for good. Evil exists in the world. People sin. Often, we do not see the full picture. Even Job, it seems, never really knew what had happened in heaven. The comfort Job received was that God finally answered him. God didn't answer all his questions, but God showed up. God was present.

Samantha Kilpatrick advises that Jesus's response should be our example:

> When an individual discloses sexual abuse, you . . . must assume a place similar to that of Christ as Immanuel (God with us). This is not the time to teach, interrogate, or investigate. This is a time to listen, to validate, and to assess what needs to happen next.[40]

As Job found, God is listening when we cry out to him. God will answer us. God cares.

You are not alone – God is with you

Perhaps no one else was there when you were abused. Perhaps, just as Job felt abandoned by his own friends, no one seems to understand.

But you are not alone. Jesus is also called Immanuel – God with us. He promises us: "And surely I am with you always, to the very end of the age" (Matthew 28:20).

Psalm 139:7, 11-12 says,

> Where can I go from your Spirit?
> Where can I flee from your presence? . . .
> If I say, "Surely the darkness will hide me
> and the light become night around me,"
> even the darkness will not be dark to you;
> the night will shine like the day,
> for darkness is as light to you.

Even in the darkest places, God is with you. He has experienced the depths of that darkness too.

Jesus is called the man of sorrows. The prophet Isaiah writes about the suffering Jesus experienced. He was physically hurt: wounded, bruised, and beaten. His body was stripped naked and mocked. But the sufferings Jesus experienced were not as a result of his own sin. And so we need to emphasize that, for victims, their abuse was from someone else's sin.

"He was despised and rejected by mankind, a man of suffering, and familiar with pain" (Isaiah 53:3a). Do you feel despised or rejected? Has someone treated you as if you have little value or worth? Jesus knows how you feel. Jesus was a man who was "familiar with pain," or "acquainted with grief" (KJV). He was betrayed by the people closest to him.

Because of what he suffered, Jesus experientially understands. He can empathize deeply with what victims of sexual abuse have gone through. You see, Jesus doesn't just know his *own* suffering – he actually knows *your* suffering. The prophet also says in Isaiah 53:4, "[He] took up our pain and bore our suffering."

The NLT says, "it was our weaknesses he carried; it was our sorrows that weighed him down" (Isaiah 53:4). Jesus carries our physical weakness as well as our emotional pain. The psalmist says that Lord is the one who "heals the broken-hearted and binds up their wounds" (Psalm 147:3). This picture shows a God who brings emotional healing to the deep pain in our souls and physical healing to our bodies as he gently wraps our wounds in bandages. You can be restored to health, wholeness, and soundness again. Jesus can work the wonder of healing and restoration.

He carried our weaknesses; he took them up. This means we can bring our heavy burdens to him. He says, "Come to me, all you who are weary and burdened, and I will give you rest. Take my yoke upon you and learn from me, for I am gentle and humble in heart, and you will find rest for your souls" (Matthew 11:28-29). 1 Peter 5:7 tells us, "Cast all your anxiety on him because he cares for you."

Jesus always welcomes us to come to him with our burdens. He knows, he feels, he understands, and cares about all that we are going through. And because he knows the truth of what happened to us, he believes us.

Not only that, but he advocates for us. Jesus "always lives to intercede for [you]" (Hebrews 7:25). Jesus is praying for your healing and restoration. He is the high priest who is able to empathize with our weaknesses, so "[let] us then approach God's throne of grace with confidence, so that we may receive mercy and find grace to help us in our time of need" (Hebrews 4:16).

Whenever we are in pain, we can look to our great high priest, Jesus. He understands what we have been through and he gives us confidence to approach God. We can expect to receive grace and mercy from him!

This does not overlook the fact that there will be a need for grieving, therapy, and other means of support as you pursue healing for your brokenness and pain. However, there is hope and assurance that restoration is possible.

God will restore and bring justice

When God spoke to Job, he gave Job a tour of creation in all its wild, beautiful, and powerful splendour. God reminded Job of his power. This reminds us that, despite the evil and suffering in the world, despite the enemy's intentions to destroy us, God is still in control. God is the Almighty Creator at the beginning and he will create a new heaven and earth in the end, where everything will be restored. Revelation 21:3-4 says:

> "Look! God's dwelling-place is now among the people, and he will dwell with them. They will be his people, and God himself will be with them and be their God. 'He will wipe every tear from their eyes. There will be no more death' or mourning or crying or pain, for the old order of things has passed away."

In the end, God restored Job's fortunes and rebuked his friends. God will act for justice. Jesus is coming again to make all things right and to judge all people. He has the final say. My friend struggled with the realization that a headmaster had sexually abused pupils and all attempts to bring him to justice had failed. She found comfort in Psalm 94, quoted in part below, which reassures us that God will eventually judge:

> The Lord is a God who avenges.
> O God who avenges, shine forth.
> Rise up, Judge of the earth;
> pay back to the proud what they deserve.
> How long, Lord, will the wicked,
> how long will the wicked be jubilant? . . .
>
> They crush your people, Lord;
> they oppress your inheritance . . .
> They say, "The Lord does not see;
> the God of Jacob takes no notice."
>
> Take notice, you senseless ones among the people;
> you fools, when will you become wise?
> Does he who fashioned the ear not hear?
> Does he who formed the eye not see?

Does he who disciplines nations not punish?
    Does he who teaches mankind lack knowledge? . . .

For the Lord will not reject his people;
    he will never forsake his inheritance.
Judgment will again be founded on righteousness,
    and all the upright in heart will follow it . . .
    I would soon have dwelt in the silence of death.
When I said, "My foot is slipping,"
    your unfailing love, Lord, supported me.
When anxiety was great within me,
    your consolation brought me joy . . .

The wicked band together against the righteous
    and condemn the innocent to death.
But the Lord has become my fortress,
    and my God the rock in whom I take refuge.

Lament

Job serves as an example for us because he expressed his distress to God honestly, just like the psalmists and even Tamar. One way to find God's "grace to help us in our time of need" is through the process of grieving and lament. Some survivors may have trouble grieving for their loss because they feel that believers should have victory in Jesus over their trauma and grief. But this is not a healthy way of dealing with pain and loss.

Part of our care for those who have been abused is to help them to grieve their abuse in a healthy and redemptive way. From her own experience, Jan Morrison (no relation to me) speaks to survivors about understanding the importance of the grieving process when she writes,

> Grieving the loss of your childhood is an important step in your journey. Acknowledge you hurt. Don't be afraid of your anger – being angry over what has been done to you is perfectly normal and acceptable. And don't be ashamed to cry! Crying over the pain can move you through your sexual abuse into a healthy view of yourself and your relationships. You can't accept the full truth about your abuse until you mourn what

> you lost as a result of your abuse. So allow yourself whatever time it takes to get through your grieving process.[41]

One manner of grieving is through the practice of lament, which can be a path to spiritual wholeness and health for someone who has experienced the evil of child sexual abuse. It is a way to survive spiritually and emotionally and helps us to focus on God and to look to a hopeful future. This may seem contradictory as we stand amid the ruins of a shattered life, desolate and seemingly with no hope for the future. And yet, when we look at the Psalms of Lament, most of them, although expressing the depths of despair, ultimately end up with expressions of hope and even joy. Rev Dr Ian Duffield comments,

> Lament then is an act of truthfulness in various ways: a naming of destructive events; an expression of pain and anger and grief; an articulation of tension and confusion; a language for tears and inexplicable emotions; a naming of errors, failures, and injustice; a personal and political resistance to the way things are; a challenge to God; a desperate cry of hope in the midst of tragedy and loss, as we dare to keep faith with God.[42]

Thus, in lament, we bring our grief, pain, anger, frustration, confusion, and any other emotion we may feel, and express them openly to God. But this is not simply a venting process. If we bring up only our pain and anger and don't focus on God by approaching the throne of grace, we end up carrying a burden that is too heavy to bear. Thus, our spiritual and emotional energy is sapped by this problem-focused response and so leads to discouragement and feeling overwhelmed. Lament must be God-focused, turning over everything that we have expressed to his loving and compassionate care.

In Psalms of Lament, we often see several key components which can help us to express our lament to God. A possible outline one could use is the following:[43]

- Address to God (Oh God . . .)
- Review of God's faithfulness in the past
- The complaint
- The confession of sin or claim of innocence

- A request for help
- God's response (or the response that is hoped for)
- A vow to praise, statement of trust in God.

For example, I have adapted the lament in Psalm 10 as "A Sexual Abuse Victim's Prayer for Help and Justice" at the end of this chapter.

This grieving and restoration process should not happen in a vacuum. It is extremely important that the church be involved in providing pastoral care and practical support and assistance for victims and their families. In doing so, they, as children of the king, will be doing what was prayed for King Solomon in Psalm 72:4, 12-14:

> May he defend the afflicted among the people
> and save the children of the needy;
> may he crush the oppressor . . .
>
> For he will deliver the needy who cry out,
> the afflicted who have no one to help.
> He will take pity on the weak and the needy
> and save the needy from death.
> He will rescue them from oppression and violence,
> for precious is their blood in his sight.

While matters of abuse are often kept confidential, there are times when the perpetrator must be publicly disciplined. In these cases, the congregation can join in the lament over the injustice. Mike Edmondson, himself a pastor, writes,

> Give the congregation something to do. Be sure to encourage them to mourn with those who mourn, to pray that God's justice will be established, God's truth will be revealed, that sin and injuries will be healed, that peace, purity, and unity will be granted to the congregation through this.[44]

This will direct the congregation's emotional and spiritual energy towards productive service and mutual support as they work through their sorrow and grief of what they have learned and experienced at the disclosure of abuse. In this way, they will be following Paul's advice to "make every effort to do what leads to peace and to mutual edification" (Romans 14:19).

A Prayer for Help and Justice

(My Adaptation of Psalm 10 for Victims of Sexual Abuse)

Why, Lord, do you stand far off?
Why do you hide yourself in the times of my trouble?

In his arrogance my wicked abuser has hunted me down.
I am weak and have been caught in the schemes he devises.
He boasts about the cravings of his heart;
in all his lusting there is no room for God . . .

His mouth is full of lies and threats against me;
trouble and evil are under his tongue.
He lies in wait near the villages;
from ambush he destroys the innocent.
His eyes watch in secret for his victims;
like a lion in cover he has lain waiting;
planning to catch me in my helplessness;
he has ensnared me and drags me off in his net.
He has crushed me, overpowering me so I collapse;
and helpless have fallen under his strength.
He thinks he can get away with his abuse and says to himself,
"God will never notice;
he covers his face and never sees."

Arise, Lord! Lift up your hand, O God.
Do not forget me for I am helpless.
But you, God, see my trouble and my affliction;
you consider my grief and take it in hand.
Oh Lord, I commit myself to you;
you are my helper.
Break the grip of my abuser;
call this evildoer to account for his wickedness
that would not otherwise be found out.

You, Lord, hear the desire of the afflicted;
encourage me, and listen to my cry for escape and justice;
defend me against my abuser for I am oppressed,
so that he will never again strike terror in my heart.

Arise, Lord! Do not forget me for I am helpless.
Oh Lord, I commit myself to you;
you are my helper.

From *Safe! How You Can Protect Children from Sexual Abuse* I © Philip E. Morrison I Published by Oasis International Ltd.

PART III

Church Discipline and Justice

7

Reporting Abuse to Authorities

Someone wanting to report child sexual abuse may not know who to approach. Their priority will often be to find someone they trust, someone they feel will believe them and be able to act. However, the person who hears the report might not know what to do about a situation of abuse.

Who to talk to first

Within your home, identify one or more support person(s) for each member of the family to talk to if there is a concern. Having a safe, responsible, and consistent adult for a child or adolescent to turn to is critical and will encourage early reporting if something does happen to the child.

In your organization, choose someone to be your child safety officer. In any cases of abuse, this person will be responsible to follow up with the proper local church, denominational, and governmental officials. In addition, this is the person who assists the victim and family in receiving spiritual, medical, legal, financial, protective, and counselling assistance through the church and social agency resources.

This designated child safety officer should have received at least the minimal training offered in this book as well as further training on child safety measures if possible. In an NGO, the child safety officer should not be the top leader. They should, ideally, be someone in human resources who has authority to act on personnel matters. Equally, in the church, the child safety officer should not be the pastor or part of the official church leadership. This is to help maintain objectivity and accountability outside the congregational authority structure. However, when and if appropriate, this person would inform the pastor of any abuse reports that may be received. If it is alleged that the pastor has been involved in the abuse, the church child safety officer should report the incident directly to a higher denominational church official.

A situation of abuse might come to the attention of a child safety officer from a member of the organization, from the person who has been abused, or from someone close to the victim. Often, this will be a verbal conversation. The child safety officer should then follow up with the person in order to document their report in writing in as much detail as possible. This is important evidence for future church discipline, termination of employment, or legal proceedings. You may use the Abuse Incident Report at the end of this chapter as a template. The child safety officer would keep all abuse reports in a confidential and safe location.

Should the victim first confront the perpetrator?

Some Christians feel that, from a biblical perspective, the victim should go to the perpetrator and confront him or her before reporting the abuse to the church or before the church takes further action. This idea is based on a misapplication of Matthew 18:15-20. Matthew 18 tells someone who has been sinned against to directly confront the person in sin, and then take a witness to confront the offender together, and finally to bring the matter to the elders.

Matthew 18, however, covers interpersonal conflict where it is possible and appropriate for the offended to confront the offender in private. It is most appropriate when no one's safety is at risk and there is a roughly equal power dynamic between the offended person and the offender. Child sexual abuse is not an interpersonal conflict – it is a crime of violent violation of the powerful against the powerless. The Bible emphasizes the protection of those who are weak and vulnerable, and in many cases, it would not be safe for those who have been sexually abused to privately confront the perpetrator. Many victims would be reluctant or fearful to personally confront the very person who had abused and traumatized them. In fact, that could further traumatize them. Boz Tchividjian, a lawyer and the founder of a ministry that responds to child abuse reports, says, "Child sexual abuse does not even fit into the paradigm of which

Jesus was speaking about in this passage. Jesus never intended these statements to be twisted into the required method for handling murder, rape, torture, kidnapping, or genocide."[45]

By misapplying the Matthew 18 process, church leadership would only cause further pain and damage to the victim. A biblical procedure that would cause harm cannot be exercised as an act of love. Insisting that the victim confront the perpetrator before any other action can be taken would effectively derail the process and allow the perpetrator to escape the consequences of their action.

Even as we deal with the perpetrator, we must keep in mind that whatever we do we cannot cause further harm or traumatization to the one they have abused. As in everything else we have discussed in this book, the welfare and care of the victim of child sexual abuse must take priority. Once what is best for the abused is established as the guiding principle, then how we deal with the perpetrator will naturally follow. What is best for the child will ultimately lead us to do what is best for the church, the perpetrator, and all those affected by the fallout of the abuse.

How to investigate reported abuse

Suppose someone comes to the child safety officer to report abuse. How does one know what action to take after the report has been documented? The child safety officer should first determine whether there is a reasonable probability that the incident took place. False accusations are rare, but they do occur. Let's look at some scenarios that illustrate how this should be determined. These stories are written as if the reader is the child safety officer.

SCENARIO 1: THE CHOIR LEADER

A 12-year-old girl tells you, the child safety officer, that last Friday evening the choir leader called on her to help put some equipment away. She related that while she was in the storeroom he came in, closed the door, grabbed her hands, and forced her to grope his crotch area. He told her to keep quiet about the matter and that if she did say something nobody would believe her. He said she should not wear such tight clothing.

You bring in the pastor's wife and listen to the girl in a quiet place. You are supportive, non-judgemental, and impartial. You ask her to point out the location where it happened. You write the full story down, including the date and time of the incident. To gain a complete picture of what took place, you ask additional questions such as, "Was anyone else around? Has it ever happened before?" You can also ask for specific facts that could be independently verified such as, "What objects did you see in the storeroom? What was he wearing?"

Then you ask to meet with the choir leader, along with a third party. When you meet, you explain that there has been a complaint by a girl in the church, but without naming the girl. The choir leader flatly denies that anything happened. He shares that he often gets kids to help him put the equipment away and says he goes in with them to instruct on where things go. Again, he insists that he has never done what he is accused of.

In this situation, we have one person's word against the other. How do you weigh up the truth?

First, in the interview, look at body language and how the accused acts and behaves when confronted. Sometimes, there may be certain clues in their facial expressions or body posture as well as the language they use that indicate whether they are telling the truth or not.

Secondly, ask yourself, "What is the general character of the individuals involved?"

Does the girl have a history of making unfounded allegations? What did she know or feel about the choir leader beforehand? Did she tell anyone else at the time? What was the impact on her? How did it make her feel? What does she need or want to happen now?

Does the choir leader have a history of inappropriate sexual conduct? In the interview, you would ask him, "What do you do to ensure you don't get into a situation where you could be misunderstood? Can you think of any motives that may have led her to say this about you?"

Based on the information you received from the interviews, you would arrive at some possible outcomes.

One outcome would be that you think the girl has malicious motives and you believe the choir leader. This would be because his character has never been called into question before, or you might discover that something happened between the choir leader and the girl that has affected her view of him. For example, he did not give her the solo that she wanted or had to discipline her for her bad behaviour.

Another outcome would be that you believe the girl and suspect that the choir leader is lying. Her story sounds credible. For instance, choir practice was going on at that time and her description of the storeroom was accurate. You also know that the girl is known to be someone who tells the truth. There is no reason to think she is lying because children do not usually make up stories like this without some foundation.

Since forced sexual touch is illegal, consider whether the girl and her parents want to pursue a police report. If they do, you can support them in that with the information you have gathered.

If this is a one-time occurrence without further evidence, it may be difficult for the police to pursue the matter further. However, by documenting the case you create a record that will give weight to possible future complaints.

Either way, you can still take your own measures to ensure that this does not happen again. Make it absolutely clear to the choir leader that he has placed himself in a very risky situation. Advise him to never go into a room with young people on his own and always have other adults present. Communicate clearly that violations of this policy or any further complaints will be taken very seriously. If the choir leader had already been trained on policies (such as increasing visibility or the two-person rule discussed in Chapter 12), appropriate disciplinary action can be taken.

You can also advise, reassure, and support the girl in self-protection. Thank her for speaking up. Tell her that you have made very clear to the choir director that he is not allowed to be alone with any child. Help her to think through what she would do if this happened again. Assure her that she can refuse any similar requests and report them to you. In case you are not available, help her think through another safe person to talk to. You can also ask her if she wants to continue to be part of the choir or what other assistance she might want.

SCENARIO 2: A CHILDREN'S HOME

You run a children's home. One of the younger boys, aged 10, comes to you in distress. He says that a group of older boys jumped on him last night and sodomised him. His shorts are torn and bloody. He is shaking with fear. You suspect this has happened before because other younger boys have had bloodied shorts but have stayed silent. Because this activity is illegal, you immediately report it to the authorities.

What might happen as a result of your report? First, the police could come and question all the boys. Suppose that when this happens, the 10-year-old retracts his testimony and the older boys deny it. Or when the police come to question the boys, the 10-year-old tells what happened and then is taken for a medical exam that confirms sodomy. Some of the older boys deny but others confess and those involved are taken into remand.

If some of the suspected boys are not taken into custody because the police determine there is not enough evidence, you can still put into place strict measures to keep younger boys away from the older boys. Make it clear that any violation of these boundaries will be punished. Secondly, provide special protection and support and counselling for the 10-year-old, who is now at great risk. Since the safety of the child is the highest value, it may be necessary to have the 10-year-old and the older boys living in different children's homes. Typically the person causing harm should be the one who experiences consequences for their actions rather than causing significant disruption to the victim's life. However, if it is not possible to move several children given limited children's homes nearby, relocating the 10-year-old may be a more realistic option.

In broader terms, you would want to provide child safety education to the residents of the children's home. You would evaluate and put into place closer supervision of the boys' dormitories to prevent a reoccurrence of this activity with anyone else. This would include making sure that there is a child safety policy in place for all the children in the home.

SUMMARY

With these scenarios as background, let us look at what does not count as a reason to dismiss an accusation as improbable. How does one tell whether something did happen when there is no hard evidence? Look at all the evidence you have gathered and evaluate it by first listing all the reasons this allegation might be true. Then evaluate the evidence by listing all the reasons it may be fabricated. This will help guide you as you move to the next step in your analysis.

Evaluate the testimony of the victim. What is the history of their character and tendency to tell the truth or lie? Did the victim offer a convincing and consistent narrative? Do the details add up? Are the places, people present, and circumstances accurate? Does the timeline fit together and support the narrative? Are there inconsistencies or contradictions in what they have said? For example, if it is alleged that the incident took place in the shower block but you know the shower block is being rebuilt, this inconsistency may cause you to question the testimony.

Are there witnesses or other individuals who are able to validate certain details of the story? Are there contradictions in the two stories that you can fact check against other sources? For instance, in the first example, suppose the choir director said he put the items away by himself. If other children confirm that the girl went to put items away after choir and the door shut behind them, that is different than if they say the girl left choir before they did.

If the matter is unclear and places one person's word against another, then all you can do is look at all the factors that led this to be an allegation and that cannot be proven or disproven. For example, the alleged incident happened in isolation and there was no accountability by the offender to other adults or staff members in their interaction with the child.

In the table below, we summarise this discussion of weighing up the balance of probability that incident occurred.

Weighing up the balance of probabilities	
Innocent?	**Guilty?**
Known good character of accused	Questionable character of accused (not trustworthy in other areas, for example, sexual unfaithfulness)
Accused is known to be honest	Accused known to tell lies, to exaggerate, to avoid responsibility
Victim is known to tell lies, to exaggerate, to avoid responsibility	Victim is known to be honest
Victim has potentially ulterior motives	Victim has no motive; good character is known
No previous allegations against accused; previous questionable accusations made by victim	Previous complaints or rumours about conduct of accused
No evidence at all	Physical evidence or circumstantial evidence (time, location, and description match)
Body language and demeanour when confronted indicate openness	Body language and demeanour when confronted indicate that they are covering up, minimizing, deflecting
Attitude of concern and shock when confronted	Defensive and blame-shifting when confronted

As you weigh these testimonies, be aware of who has the power in the situation. You must not be swayed by the status of the accused! Be careful not to side with the alleged offender by saying, “There is no proof, so we believe you.”

Be careful not to shame the alleged victim through interrogation. Listen supportively and ask questions gently. While the person receiving the disclosure from the child such as a parent or teacher would say, “I believe you”, the child safety officer who is interviewing should not. Your role is to gather information and be impartial. You can encourage them to speak by saying, “You are brave”, “I am really glad that you are sharing this”, “I don’t want you to be afraid”, or “You can say anything, and I won’t be angry.”

Make the welfare of the victim central. Give the highest priority to caring for the child’s immediate needs and the needs of the family. We have discussed these steps in the previous chapters.

There are cases where touch may have been unwanted and inappropriate, but it is not illegal. For instance, hugs or other touch that is not explicitly sexual may still make a child uncomfortable. If the action is not illegal, then look at how this happened and put in place safeguards moving forward to prevent any likelihood of misunderstanding. Emphasise that the alleged offender needs to avoid any future situations that would raise suspicions about their action and motives. If the action is illegal, consider reporting to the police, but bear in mind the risk to the victim. If you know that the system will traumatize the child even further or put them at risk, then consider the best course of action with the victim's best interests at heart. If a serious crime, such as rape, is alleged then you should consider passing the matter on to authorities regardless of your assessment of the credibility of the report.

Take quick legal action

Once the initial report has been made to the child safety officer and determined credible and the conduct illegal, the organization should not delay in addressing this issue with the perpetrator and the law. All of these steps should be taken immediately after receiving a report of abuse.

Call your church or organization's attorney. No matter what level of understanding of the law your leadership may have, it is imperative to obtain legal counsel so that proper procedures and protections for the organization may be put into place.

Immediately put the perpetrator on administrative leave. This means that the perpetrator is required to cease any and all contact with children and involvement in children's ministries. Practically speaking, this means that the perpetrator would not be allowed to enter the building or compound of your church or organization. Not to do so may expose children to further risk and traumatization and could make yourselves legally liable.

Report the abuse to the appropriate governmental authorities. This means that the leadership should research the laws regarding reporting procedures and to which entities the report should be made. This will bring you into compliance with the law and turn over the investigation to those in the authoritative position to do so.

Inform the perpetrator of the above actions and advise him or her to contact an attorney. This demonstrates that you are taking the report of abuse seriously, but also shows the perpetrator that you care for his or her welfare. By handling this properly, you do not forfeit your shepherding role and you open the door for the future ministry of redemption and reconciliation.

Is it necessary to report sexual abuse?

Once these immediate steps have been taken, there are two routes to pursue simultaneously towards achieving justice for the victim: the local church should exercise church discipline for those who have been involved in sexual misconduct, and sexual abuse should be reported to the civil authorities in accordance with the law. Those who are involved in child sexual abuse are not only breaking the law of God, but also the laws of the land. Therefore, as soon as abuse of a child is disclosed, the process of church discipline and the legal process should begin.

My research showed that about a third (38 per cent) of respondents saw perpetrators disciplined by the church, 18 saw discipline only at the local church level, 7 saw discipline only at the denominational level, and 13 saw discipline at both levels. Two-thirds of respondents saw the church report child sexual abuse to the police or social service authorities. This is a good start, but there is room for improvement.

Sadly, it is true that governmental authorities may not take cases of child abuse seriously. Denis McCrann comments on the situation in Tanzania: "The legal system does not handle cases of child sexual abuse with sufficient care. For example, paying a small fee to the family of the victim settles the problem in the short term but the perpetrator is free to continue abusing other children. In addition, in cases that do make it to court, the child is treated like an adult."[46] Children are easily intimidated and need specialist interviewing and representation. A child who is victimized cannot be expected to go through the court process as an adult would. This simply leads to retraumatization. If you can, find a counsellor familiar with the court process to help children in taking the matter to court.

However, if the church or NGO does not report child sexual abuse to the authorities, they are involved in a cover-up of a crime and are guilty of enabling the perpetrator to continue the abuse. It is only by bringing the perpetrator to justice that justice can be gained for the victim. So reporting to the local government is necessary, but it is only part of the intervention. Church discipline is also essential, and NGOs can follow up with the offender's local congregation to initiate that process.

Some might object that bringing to justice a church member or a family member may be harsh and unloving. First of all, working to bring justice to the victim is an essential part of loving the victim. Without justice, the relational wound is left open and long-term healing for the victim will be difficult. In the book *Sexually Exploited Children: Working to Protect and Heal,* Phyllis Kilbourn writes, "Children have a strong sense of justice, and the prosecution of the perpetrator can satisfy this basic need . . . they can find such action strengthening and therapeutic."[47]

But bringing justice is also being loving to a perpetrator. Victoria Johnson, in her book, *Children and Sexual Abuse,* says:

> It may be only during incarceration or court proceedings that offenders get the help they need. Offenders should continue to receive spiritual support from the church – especially if the family is too emotionally shattered to support them.[48]

As we discuss below, support for a perpetrator does not mean restoration to their former position or ministry. Nor does it mean attendance at services without certain guidelines in place restricting their access to children. However, support could also include prayer, providing counselling, and if possible, the process of forgiveness and restoration of the relationship that may need to take place over a long period.

A biblical response to child abuse demands that we administer justice for both the victim and perpetrator. Walter Brueggemann says justice "is active intervention to transform society . . . to act favourably toward the weak and, on the other hand, effectively against the abusive wrong."[49] If there is any hope for healing for the child and change for the perpetrator, we must respond to the abuse and bring the perpetrator to account for his or her abusive actions. The next chapter shows us what this justice looks like.

Abuse Incident Report

All information included here will be treated with the utmost confidentiality. You will not be quoted unless permission is received from you ahead of time. We appreciate you helping us to document this incident from your point of view while the memory is fresh.

When completed, this report should immediately be turned in to the designated church child safety officer.

1. Details of Incident	
Date of Incident	
Time of incident	
Location of incident	
Who was involved?	
2. Were there other children present?	
3. Description of incident	
What happened and how it happened. Please note any conditions that may have contributed to the incident. If more room is needed, please use the other side.	

From *Safe! How You Can Protect Children from Sexual Abuse* | © Philip E. Morrison | Published by Oasis International Ltd.

From *Safe! How You Can Protect Children from Sexual Abuse* | © Philip E. Morrison | Published by Oasis International Ltd.

3.1. If there were witnesses, please include their name and phone number.

3.2. Who else was notified of the incident at the time: (children's pastor, office secretary, church administrator, senior pastor, emergency personnel, etc.).

4. What actions were taken?

5. Follow up: Who followed up the following day?

6. What was the parents' response?

Signature:	
Date:	
Phone number:	

From *Safe! How You Can Protect Children from Sexual Abuse* I © Philip E. Morrison I Published by Oasis International Ltd.

8

Pursuing Justice

In 2008 Gregory Dow and his wife, Mary Rose, both from the United States, founded the Dow Family Children's Home in Boito, Kenya. It was to be a place of ministry and hope for the 80 children in the orphanage and where they would be given food, housing, and education. However, for 10 years the Dows physically and sexually abused the children.[50]

While they provided social services, it was also found that children often went to bed hungry. Punishments included children confined to a corner with soap in their mouths. Dow began sexually assaulting some of the girls and his wife took the girls to a doctor to have birth-control devices implanted without their consent. When two girls reported him to the authorities in 2017, Dow fled back to the US to escape prosecution in Kenya.

This story is a tragic example of abuse and injustice. What makes it even worse is that in 1996, Gregory Dow had pleaded guilty to sexually assaulting another young girl in the US, yet churches that knew about this situation still supported his work in Kenya.

Micah 6:8: asks, "And what does the Lord require of you? To act justly and to love mercy and to walk humbly with your God." James 4:17 says, "If anyone, then, knows the good they ought to do and doesn't do it, it is sin for them". To remain quiet when we encounter abuse is to be guilty of passively participating in it. When we see injustice, God requires us to act and intervene in kindness and humility.

Sexual violence in Judges

There are many biblical references that call out to us as God's people to become involved in issues of justice. However, I want to look at the biblical example in Judges 20 where we have the aftermath of the horribly disturbing story of sexual violence that led to the death of a young woman. While not specifically about child sexual abuse, there are lessons from this story that tell us about the importance of dealing with sexual violence within the church.

The story begins with a Levite whose concubine runs away and returns to her home. He goes to bring her back and, after staying a number of days feasting with his father-in-law, he begins the journey home. It is late afternoon when they decide to stay overnight in the Benjaminite town of Gibeah. The men of the town come to the house where he has been invited to stay for the night and ask to have homosexual relations with him. Rather than agree, the Levite betrays his concubine and gives her to them. They abuse her sexually all night. In the morning, when he is ready to leave, he finds her dead on the doorstep. He takes her body back home, cuts her into 12 pieces, and sends one piece to each tribe.

The Levite's gruesome treatment of the concubine's body – as if she were an animal being butchered – is a dramatic and graphic illustration of how the men of Gibeah viewed her as less than human. It is shockingly violent – just as their violation of her had been. The Levite's action demanded that Israel act and the whole nation was summoned to go up against Gibeah in judgement against them. We read this in Judges 20:12-14:

> The tribes of Israel sent messengers throughout the tribe of Benjamin, saying, "What about this awful crime that was committed among you? Now turn those wicked men of Gibeah over to us so that we may put them to death and purge the evil from Israel." But the Benjaminites would not listen to their fellow Israelites. From their towns they came together at Gibeah to fight against the Israelites.

They call for the perpetrators to be handed over, but the tribe of Benjamin refuses. This triggers the war that almost wipes out their whole tribe.

Notice that the nation's purpose in going to war with the tribe of Benjamin was to purge evil from Israel. We may find that interesting since Israel had long been committing evil by turning away from God and following the idolatrous practices of the Canaanites. But this act of sexual violence and murder went too far even for their very low standards. In Judges 19:30 we see the horrified response of the nation: "Such a thing has never been seen or done, not since the day the Israelites came up out of Egypt. Just imagine! We must do something! So speak up!"

Take away the perpetrator's power and position

This intervention of the nation of Israel is in line with Job's description of his response to injustice: "I broke the fangs of the wicked and snatched the victims from their teeth" (Job 29:17). William Reyburn comments, "To break the fangs of an animal is to disable it so that it is largely defenceless and unable to capture its victim."[51] Therefore, Job is saying he not only rescued the oppressed, but he also disabled the oppressor so that he could not continue committing his crimes. This is what the nation of Israel was doing.

If we apply this to our day, preventing continuing predation on old and new victims must be one of the main purposes of the church's intervention.

We need more leaders to step forward like the pastor who took immediate action in a situation of abuse in the Sunday school. One of the teachers lost her temper with a young boy who was not listening. She grabbed the child by the hair and dragged him out of the room and shouted at him. The child ran into church crying.

After the service there was a meeting with the boy's parents and the pastor apologized and assured them that they would meet with the Sunday-school teacher and the other teachers too. The matter was then addressed in depth by the pastoral team to uncover more about what happened and what needed to be done. Meanwhile, the teacher was given six months off from teaching Sunday school in order to rest and reflect. The Sunday-school team drew up some guidelines for teachers and conducted a day's seminar on safety and effective teaching strategies.

While this was physical abuse rather than sexual abuse, the church's quick response was commended. If this had been sexual abuse, the response would have been quite different as the Sunday-school teacher would have been removed from her position immediately and civil authorities would have been informed and the legal process followed. In both cases, the action was to take away the power and position of the teacher, so that they could not continue to be used for abuse.

What pleases God is seen in Isaiah 58:6: "Is not this the kind of fasting I have chosen: to loose the chains of injustice and untie the cords of the yoke, to set the oppressed free and break every yoke?" God's people are called to loosen chains and break yokes. Making things right means undoing the tools that were used to hurt people and set them free.

Jeremiah writes, "This is what the Lord says: do what is just and right. Rescue from the hand of the oppressor the one who has been robbed" (Jeremiah 22:3a). The passage tells of those who had been robbed of finances. But this principle of intervention is applicable to the victims of child sexual abuse who have been robbed of their innocence, dignity, and, at times, their virginity. When we know a child is in an abusive situation, we need to remove them from that setting and provide a safe place for them to recover physically, spiritually, and emotionally. We must rescue children who are being sexually abused.

One example of rescuing girls is that of the New Scent Centre in Machakos County of Kenya. Flora Mwikali founded it in 2015 when she became aware of the abuse of girls living on the streets in her town. They survived mainly by sleeping with men who would buy them a little food and have sex with them in return. For lack of any other kind of shelter, a group of girls slept amid the sand heaps and this is also where some of the men would lay with the girls, while others spent their nights in trash bins within the market. Some of the other girls who were not on the streets were being abused at home, especially by their fathers, or were at risk.

By faith, Flora began to care for 11 girls. Since then, the centre has continued to grow in the number they care for, providing safety, shelter, food, medical attention, and education for girls who were victims of sexual abuse.[52]

What is our response when we hear of child sexual abuse in our churches? How do we respond when we know of pastors and church leaders in our congregations who are perpetrators of child sexual abuse? Do we say, "We must do something"? Do we speak up? Do we rescue victims? Do we take their power away so they cannot continue to harm people? Or do we respond as the tribe of Benjamin?

Do not protect the perpetrator

How did the tribe of Benjamin respond? When asked to turn over the perpetrators to face the consequences of their wicked acts, they refused. They would not listen to those who were asking them to do what was right. When we refuse to confront sin and the sinners in our midst, we give their sin our approval. In fact, when we as church leaders refuse to discipline those in our midst who commit child sexual abuse, we are in fact guilty of participating in their sin ourselves. We become like the church that supported the Dows in their work with Kenyan children even though they knew of his past sexual assault.

The tribe of Benjamin compounded their sin by actually defending the perpetrators of sexual abuse as they came together at Gibeah to fight the Israelites. *The Life Application Study Bible* note on this passage has a very insightful comment:

> They would not listen to the rest of Israel and hand over the accused criminals. They were more loyal to their own tribe than to God's law. By covering for their kinsmen, the entire tribe of Benjamin sank to the level of immorality as low as that of the criminals. Through this act, we get a glimpse of how thoroughly the nation's moral fabric had unraveled.[53]

What does it say about the unravelling of our churches' moral fabric when we refuse to deal with and discipline our pastors, church leaders, and members when they commit sexual abuse? We are just as guilty as the tribe of Benjamin when we cover up the child sexual abuse in our midst and defend the perpetrators by simply transferring them somewhere else or by refusing to initiate church discipline.

I see many parallels in this story with the present situation of unaddressed child sexual abuse in our churches. For example, after a Sunday-school camp weekend was over, two girls told their parents that a youth leader had come into the bathroom when they were bathing and taken a photo of them with his phone. The parents went to the pastor to tell him. He said that the youth leader was a nephew of the senior elder and that he would tell the elder to ask his nephew to delete the images. The pastor asked the parents not to mention this to anyone. Although the parents were unhappy with this plan, they felt silenced by the pastor. In the meantime, the youth leader continued in his ministry as usual.

A friend of mine who works at a children's home in Africa told me, "We have fired staff in leadership positions at our homes for sexual abuse allegations we found to be true. They have been pastors or elders in our denomination. We have notified the church; and they continue to be in their positions of authority within the church. It's sickening."

In Psalm 82:2-4, God holds rulers accountable for their failure to protect the innocent:

> How long will you defend the unjust
> 	and show partiality to the wicked?
> Defend the weak and the fatherless;
> 	uphold the cause of the poor and the oppressed.
> Rescue the weak and the needy;
> 	deliver them from the hand of the wicked.

Allowing incidences such as these to happen and failing to address them is an indication of the moral corruption and decay in our midst. How long before we experience and see God's hand of judgement upon us and those who refuse to purge evil from our midst but instead cover up and defend the perpetrators?

Fighting injustice is costly

What happened to the tribe of Benjamin? At first, it seemed that their defence would be successful. For two days, and in two battles, they withstood the attacks of the other tribes. In fact, the other tribes of Israel lost 40,000 men! And so I must point out here that often the battle to do what is right is not easy. It is going to be costly. Even though they asked the Lord for guidance at the beginning of their action against the wickedness of Benjamin, they suffered loss!

Even though we are doing what is right, it is going to cost us. In Isaiah 58:7, God's people are enjoined to "share your food with the hungry and to provide the poor wanderer with shelter – when you see the naked, to clothe them." In James 2:15-16, the apostle says, "Suppose a brother or sister is without clothes and daily food. If one of you says to them, 'Go in peace; keep warm and well fed,' but does nothing about their physical needs, what good is it?" Thus, when we think of intervening in situations of child sexual abuse we need to be prepared that it will cost us our time, finances, and emotional and spiritual energy.

While we may not go to war like the Israelites, if we are going to confront sexual abuse, we must be prepared for a battle. When we are doing God's will the forces of evil will fiercely resist us. Those who should be seeking justice for the victim often ignore, belittle, deny, or cover up the sin. Police and judges may be corrupt or incompetent, and the trial process can take years as the case makes its way through the court system. The powerful may find ways to bribe officials or threaten victims.

It is at times like this that the survivor of abuse may question whether pressing charges and taking the case forward is worth the emotional pain and struggle. This is a valid question and the survivor will need to choose the way forward that best fits their situation, since their well-being is the primary concern. However, as Christians receiving a report or supporting and advocating for someone else, we should not place the cost to ourselves and the risks involved above pursuing justice on their behalf.

It is important to note that although the tribes were facing fierce opposition, they did not quit. After suffering the loss of so many men, they might have given up, but they didn't. Instead, they continued to seek the Lord. Look at Judges 20:26-28:

> Then all the Israelites, the whole army, went up to Bethel, and there they sat weeping before the Lord. They fasted that day until evening and presented burnt offerings and fellowship offerings to the Lord. And the Israelites enquired of the Lord. (In those days the ark of the covenant of God was there, with Phinehas son of Eleazar, the son of Aaron, ministering before it.) They asked, "Shall we go up again to fight against the Benjaminites, our fellow Israelites, or not?" The Lord responded, "Go, for tomorrow I will give them into your hands."

And so, with the Lord's reassurance and encouragement, they were ultimately successful, and the tribe of Benjamin was severely punished.

We must be realistic that, in our broken world, justice is not always accomplished or perfectly achieved. Yet pursuing justice can be an encouragement to other victims, and empower them to disclose and report their own abuse. It can also be a means to prevent further abuse by perpetrators as they are dealt with by the authorities.

Sin is messy, and it is costly to clean up the mess. And yet that is what God calls us to do. We must be committed to bearing the cost on behalf of those who have suffered trauma and abuse. We must be prepared to bear the cost of dealing with those who have committed the sin of sexual abuse. It will not be easy, but it is what God calls us to do.

Where are the men and women who will come forward and courageously confront those in power who refuse to deal with the wickedness of child sexual abuse in their midst? Who will confront those who, for the sake of power and position, cover over the sin – and even defend the evildoers?

Let's return to the tragic tale of the orphanage where Gregory and Mary Rose Dow abused children. Fortunately, the story did not end there. Margaret Ruto, a Kenyan mother and nursing student living in the US, found out about the investigation through Facebook. She realized that Dow could still be convicted in the US and determined to collect as much evidence as possible. Through phone calls, working with a Kenyan lawyer, and visiting Boito to collect first-hand testimonies, she was able to provide US authorities with many leads so that they were eventually able to follow up the investigation in Kenya. Through Ruto's perseverance, Dow was sentenced to 16 years in prison in February 2021.

In a documentary on the subject, NTV journalist Edmond Nyabola said, "Those kids can finally find justice because of the good noise she made, the evidence she put together, the doors she knocked, and not to mention, the bravery to even think of taking this on . . . The people of Boito feel a sense of relief . . . [because] the wheels of justice are rolling."[54]

Margaret Ruto shows us that ordinary people can make a difference. May God raise up those who take up this battle, intervene for the sake of the victims of child sexual abuse, and stand for righteousness and justice.

9

Confession, Forgiveness, and Reconciliation

Some people may be uncomfortable with the notion of church discipline and justice. You may wonder where the idea of forgiveness fits in? When can the perpetrator be restored to ministry? The idea of forgiveness is one of the most misunderstood concepts when it comes to abuse. While we want to see care for the perpetrator, we also want to proceed with caution so that we do not retraumatize the victim in the process.

Do not pressure a victim to forgive

A common way churches encourage restoration is to urge the perpetrator to immediately ask for forgiveness and the victim to grant it. But there can be a real danger with an adult offender if he or she is offered easy forgiveness by church leadership, or the restoration process is rushed or forced upon the victim.

To avoid consequences, perpetrators may go to their pastor and ask for forgiveness. One writer says, "Because the petitioner appears remorseful and seems to be following the prescribed formula to activate God's grace, many pastors utter the words of assurance: 'You are forgiven.'"[55] This is wrong because the pastor cannot forgive on behalf of the victim and thus bypasses the victim against the direction of Scripture. If the pastor "forgives," the perpetrator can demand forgiveness by saying, "The pastor says I am forgiven, so you must forgive me."

Or, the perpetrator may rush through the process, using scriptures about forgiveness and reconciliation to avoid the consequences of their abuse and so manipulate the victim by saying, "The Bible says you should forgive. And if you forgive, you shouldn't report."

Easy forgiveness may be desired by either the perpetrator or the church leadership in order to offer a quick solution. However, the perpetrator cannot demand forgiveness, nor can the church force it; it must be freely given. Forced forgiveness does not help the perpetrator address the root causes of his sin. Pressure to quickly forgive the perpetrator shifts the focus from the victim's healing to the perpetrator's restoration. This retraumatizes the victim, telling them once again that their voice and emotions don't matter.

Forcing forgiveness is wrong because it doesn't adequately consider the cost of that forgiveness to the victim. This illustrates, as one counsellor said, that "[p]erpetrators often do not understand how long the process can take as they do not comprehend how difficult it is for the abused to come to the point where they can forgive their abuser." While forgiveness is valuable, we must recognize the breadth and complexity of the process that the perpetrator, victim, and church must go through before restoration can occur.

Jennifer Greenberg shares three negative results from pressuring the victim to grant premature forgiveness.[56] The first is that *premature forgiveness denies survivors time to process emotions.*

Some people argue, "We *know* we should forgive and so we *will* to forgive." This simplistic approach only sees forgiveness as volitional and intellectual, and suggests that as God's forgiveness is instantaneous and complete, so ours should be. However, this ignores the psychological and spiritual effects on the victim. Many victims experience a long process of internal wrestling before they can forgive because forgiveness is complex and has different levels.

Pressuring victims to forgive quickly disrespects their autonomy and is unjust. Asking the victim to offer forgiveness too early in the process, before they have adequately dealt with the anger, hatred, and the desire for vengeance upon one's enemies, is to offer a "cheap forgiveness" for the perpetrator and leaves the victim with unresolved issues of the heart.

Survivors need to be able to honestly identify and acknowledge their feelings of anger, betrayal, isolation, helplessness, hopelessness, and shame. These difficult and devastating emotions cannot be ignored and denied.

Only once they have worked through their feelings, can they begin to recover, to heal, and to overcome.

The second negative result is that *premature forgiveness puts the responsibility of reconciliation on the victim, instead of the perpetrator.* The reason the relationship has been broken is not primarily because the victim has not forgiven. It is because the perpetrator has sinned. Therefore, the perpetrator's repentance and evidence of changed behaviour are the first and most important steps if there is to be any possibility of reconciliation. Once again, forcing premature forgiveness when there is no evidence of repentance only serves to retraumatize the survivor.

The final negative result is that *premature forgiveness enables abusers.* This is especially true of those perpetrators who may have physically or emotionally abused their victim. It is hoped that a sexual perpetrator would no longer have access to the child they had abused. However, in some countries, because perpetrators are not brought to justice by legal authorities or the abuse is handled by local chiefs or privately between families, the perpetrator may still be able to interact with the victim. In cases such as these, because the perpetrators still have access to their victim, they can continue to manipulate, threaten, or control their victims because they will feel the offence is now behind him or her and that there was no real consequence for what they had done.

Forgiveness does play a large part in the victim's recovery, but it is also very difficult to achieve. As we seek to help those who have been abused, we need to compassionately help them work through their anger and walk with them through their pain until they are ready to offer forgiveness and to see it for what it really is and how they can practically live it out.

Encourage a perpetrator to confess

Before forgiveness can be given and justice achieved, the act of abuse needs to be named and acknowledged as wrong.

This important step allows the victim to clearly frame the abuse in all its horror and atrocity. The victim claims no responsibility for what was done to her. The abuse and trauma lie squarely at the perpetrator's feet. Some people confuse forgiveness with making excuses for behaviour.

We will let go of our anger because the perpetrator didn't really mean it or didn't know better, or the perpetrator had a difficult childhood, or the victim should not have been so naïve or the victim was behaving badly. For the victim to accept some fault or blame for the abuse against her, even in the very act of forgiveness, is to perpetuate the injustice against her and thus to undermine the process of justice that will lead to her healing.

As part of the church discipline process, the leadership should work with the perpetrator to seek to bring him to a point of confession. This does not mean that the child must personally confront the perpetrator – as we already know, this simply retraumatizes them – but the church leadership can take on this responsibility in light of their duty to "keep watch over" the souls of those under their care (Hebrews 13:17) and to restore those who are "caught in a sin" (Galatians 6:1).

Naming and condemning the wrong in the process of justice are equally as important for the perpetrator. He must now confess the abuse in all its horror and atrocity without excuse, rationalization, or downplaying what he has done. This is true biblical confession and must be the initial step in asking for forgiveness and bringing about justice. The Greek word for confession is ὁμολογέω (*homologeó*), which means "to speak the same, to agree." Thus, the perpetrator agrees and affirms that what he did was wrong and takes responsibility for what he has done.

How does a confession relate to justice? By admitting his evil actions, the perpetrator tacitly and openly acknowledges that he has committed a wrong that implicitly carries with it a certain penalty or punishment. And in so doing, the perpetrator submits to a penalty that will fulfil justice.

Thus, the church's role in achieving justice is to encourage a full and honest confession by the perpetrator. This is where pastoral care is important in bringing about healing and biblical reconciliation when abuse has occurred.

Does forgiveness mean a restored relationship?

Forgiveness is the victim's choice. Confession and repentance are the perpetrator's choice. A restored relationship requires both the victim and the perpetrator. But the victim can offer a certain kind of forgiveness regardless of how the perpetrator acts.

Jennifer Greenberg has defined two modes of forgiveness that offer a path that allows the victim to come to terms with their anger and the truth of their betrayal and violation. The first is "boundaried forgiveness." Greenberg defines it as follows:

> Boundaried Forgiveness [*sic*] is when we let go of our anger, resentment, and desire for revenge; yet we may maintain boundaries and pursue justice. We do not bear a grudge, but we may file a police report . . . The storm inside is quelled, but we won't tolerate further abuse . . . We aspire to let go of our anger but not our common sense.[57]

She explains that, as a first step, forgiveness could be given this way when the perpetrator remains unrepentant, and when he continues to present a threat physically, emotionally, or even spiritually. This gives the survivor time and space to deal with his or her emotions without being forced to re-enter into a relationship with the one who caused so much harm and pain.

However, there is a second mode of forgiveness, which can build upon the foundation of boundaried forgiveness, and this is what Greenberg terms "reconciled forgiveness". This mode addresses the relationship and, ultimately, some level of restoration. She describes this as:

> . . . only ideal when the abuser is genuinely repentant. Their behaviour has changed, and we've had time to objectively observe this with a clear head and a mending heart. They've given us space to grieve, they're working on making amends, and we no longer feel threatened or endangered by them. While our relationship may not be perfect or completely restored, a process toward reconciliation has begun.[58]

Theologically, we believe that if perpetrators truly repent and victims forgive the perpetrator, they can experience restoration of the relationship, but it is hard for us to feel anything but anger against those who violate children. Miroslav Volf acknowledges the difficulty of this truth when he writes, "No redeemed future is imaginable in which perpetrators – even judged and transformed perpetrators! – are dressed in white robes. Everything in us rebels against the image. Yet everything we know about the God of the cross demands that we seriously entertain it."[59]

James W. Fowler writes: "In the struggle against the structures of evil and oppressors, Christians must also struggle as those who hope for the redemption of the oppressor."[60] If we believe in the transforming message of the gospel, we must wrestle with the tension of our feelings of repugnance and revulsion towards the perpetrator and overcome our reluctance to work towards restoration of the offender and his[61] reconciliation without losing sight of our responsibility to work towards justice for both the abused and the perpetrator. When it happens, forgiveness is a wonderful thing for the offender. I remember a young boy who was involved in inappropriate child-to-child behaviour. After he confessed, his countenance changed, and he was filled with joy.

Of course, many people who abuse children sexually only pretend to repent, or never truly repent. In that case, re-establishing a relationship with the perpetrator would not be appropriate, and reconciled forgiveness is not possible.

Even in cases where reconciled forgiveness happens, this is not easily accomplished, it should not be pressured, and it is often a long journey. Often, it is not until the abused child has become an adult that they are truly able to process all the implications of what happened to them, that they are able to heal, find a restored sense of self, and choose how to forgive.

To engage in boundaried forgiveness or reconciled forgiveness, it helps to have the love and support of the body of Christ. Forgiveness is difficult on any level and the commitment to continue to forgive may waver. It is only as fellow believers – and often trained professional counsellors as well – come alongside and support the victim in the desire to first forgive and then to continue will they be able to enter into the full freedom that forgiveness gives.

When do we restore the perpetrator?

Some hold the view that it is the responsibility of individuals and churches (as a group of individuals) to forgive, and of governments to seek justice. In this way, they compartmentalize forgiveness and justice. But this view abrogates the Scriptural duty that we seek righteousness and justice and, as Christians, must actively work to bring about justice when cases of injustice have become known.

Some perpetrators feel that if they have been forgiven they should not have to suffer any consequences for their sinful behaviour. Forgiveness does not, however, eradicate consequences. When the Israelites sinned against God by refusing to go into the Promised Land, God was so angry that he wanted to destroy them. Moses pleaded with the Lord to forgive, and the Lord's response is very instructive in light of the issue of forgiveness and consequences:

> The Lord replied, "I have forgiven them, as you asked. Nevertheless, as surely as I live and as surely as the glory of the Lord fills the whole earth, not one of those who saw my glory and the signs I performed in Egypt and in the wilderness but who disobeyed me and tested me ten times – not one of them will ever see the land I promised on oath to their ancestors. No one who has treated me with contempt will ever see it (Numbers 14:20-23).

Our God is forgiving and just, and we are called to be like him.

Forgiveness and justice are connected in the process of healing and restoring relationships. When the perpetrator confesses, they acknowledge their wrong. When the victim forgives, they acknowledge their innocence and the fact that they were sinned against.

However, confessing and asking for forgiveness do not immediately or automatically requalify someone for leadership, ministry, or employment. Even forgiveness granted by a victim does not mean the perpetrator should not face the consequences of their actions. Just as it is important to avoid premature forgiveness, it is important that we avoid an early restoration to ministry.

Child sexual abuse is a serious matter, indicative of deep-rooted psychological and spiritual issues. These issues disqualify one from ministry or leadership and need to be addressed through spiritual and therapeutic counselling. Not only that, but the power and respect that comes with position are tools – tools that people can use to abuse. It is not helpful, or wise, to give these tools to individuals who have abused in the past and allow them an opportunity to use them in the same way again.

If an employee of an NGO or church commits abuse, employment needs to be terminated. There is no expectation that the perpetrator would ever be reinstated after confession or forgiveness, although personal relationships may be informally restored.

In cases where the offender is a member of a church, we need to raise the question about how to bring a sexual offender back into the fellowship and allow them to attend services. If, after confession and going through the legal processes, an offender desires to return to church, strict boundaries and requirements need to be put in place and agreed to by both the church leadership and the offender. These boundaries might include, among others, the following:

- Limiting the offender's presence at church services to the sanctuary and being restricted from places in the church compound where children are present, or children's ministries are conducted.
- Having a chaperone present with the offender at all times. This would include, but not limited to, being escorted to the sanctuary upon arrival at the church compound and to the exit upon departure.
- Arranging a specific time for the offender's arrival and departure from the church compound.
- Informing the church leadership or designated chaperone if the offender will be absent from the church service. This increases accountability and allows the chaperone to know what to expect on any given Sunday.

Putting these boundaries in place is a way the congregation can act in a loving manner towards the perpetrator, because it takes away the temptations that will be stumbling blocks for their growth. However, if the offender does not want to abide by these basic guidelines, the leadership should not allow him to attend the services of either the local church or churches under their care. These restrictions are to reassure the congregation of the commitment to child safety within their midst and that the church takes seriously the responsibility of protecting their children.

In contrast, when issues of child sexual abuse are not dealt with properly, the abuse simply continues. Think of the youth leader taking pictures of girls in the bathroom. Will he stop unless his actions are addressed? The lack of action by the church undermines confidence that the church cares, or even that God cares.

There was a youth pastor who was found to have impregnated one of the girls in the youth group. Instead of taking proper corrective discipline by removing him from the ministry, the denominational leadership moved him to another post. It was not surprising that at the new location it was later discovered that he had gotten another young girl pregnant. The same thing happened in the Gregory Dow case, where he offended in the US and continued his patterns of abuse when he moved to Kenya. In fact, it is very common that perpetrators continue their activity once they move to another place.

Having a robust approach to abuse creates confidence for victims to come forward, knowing they will be believed and that the church will do what they can to achieve justice for them and the offender.

10

A True Story

In the past few chapters, we have looked at how to report abuse and pursue justice. Of course, real-life situations are often more complicated. In this chapter, we reflect on a real account by someone, whom we will call John, who was personally involved in the church's response to a report of child sexual abuse.[62] At the time of the incident, the church did not have a child safety policy in place to guide John or the church elders in how to handle the situation. They were doing the best they could under the circumstances, but reflecting on his account offers valuable lessons for the dilemmas we might encounter and pitfalls we can avoid.

> I often ask myself if I could have done it better. If I had not been in the middle of the sad saga, I would have insisted that people were maligning my pastor. It is food for serious thought. I was involved in Christian ministry and an active member in my church but was not an elder. I was quite concerned when a young adult approached my wife and complained that Pastor Jehu had made inappropriate sexual advances to her. When my wife told me about it, I asked her to see if she would be willing to share her story with the elders. When the lady refused, my wife told her to remain quiet about it because there was nothing to be gained from her talk. This was in keeping with [my understanding at the time of] biblical rules about correcting those in the wrong. Also, as I was not part of the church leadership at the time, I [felt I] could not approach the elders without a witness [the lady who disclosed the abuse].
>
> A year later things began to unfold. We had a teens' camp that August and Pastor Jehu's daughter, Agnes, age 14, was one of the

campers. One day she made a comment to one of the ladies cooking for the teens. The lady told my wife, "This girl behaves like she's been abused." And then she added, "I hope it is not her father." I found the whole matter intriguing, but I had nothing to go on, so I let it pass.

Unbeknownst to us, Agnes had been having nightmares, and had started meeting with the school counsellor. She finally confided to the counsellor that her father had been defiling her since she was eight and had threatened to kill her, her mother, and her brothers if she ever told anyone.

The school summoned Pastor Jehu's wife, Rahab, and she sat with the school counsellor as Agnes told her story. She then took Agnes to the local Women's Hospital, where it was confirmed that she had been sexually abused. However, the gender violence counsellor told them they would not be able to sustain a case in court. Agnes told her mother to install CCTV at home, since that was where most of the abuse happened. That was done secretly.

One morning soon after, Rahab left for work at seven o'clock. Forty-five minutes later, Agnes called saying she had been raped by her father who had then left for a meeting. Rahab asked one of the ladies from the church, who lived close to them, to take Agnes to the hospital. That evening Pastor Jehu was arrested at home and locked up in jail. He was arraigned in court two days later.

When Pastor Jehu was granted bail a few days later, Rahab and the children moved to a temporary shelter provided by her employer. This is where I first visited them. In lengthy talks I told Rahab that we would not make the matter public for her and the children's sake, and especially for Agnes. I advised that it might be wise to take a break and attend church elsewhere. But the children, Agnes included, insisted that they wanted to attend church at their church. Fortunately, the matter was kept confidential and to the best of my knowledge, the majority of the people in our congregation know nothing about what happened. Rahab and the children did get professional counselling, which we had advised.

Pastor Jehu worked very hard to cover up the case against him. He went to a pastor of another church to have him put pressure on his wife, Rahab, to be quiet and not report him. The pastor called me and when I briefed him about the case, he advised that I talk to the lawyer he had recommended to Pastor Jehu and who had agreed to take the case. Apparently, Pastor Jehu had not told him the facts of the case. When I talked to the lawyer, he said he would not represent Pastor Jehu. I went to Pastor Jehu and advised him to plead guilty and ask for a psychiatric assessment, since what he had done should not be considered normal. He ignored my advice and instead went ahead to bribe the court officials. When his case went before the magistrate, he failed to appear in court and went into hiding.

One of the problems I faced with the elders is confidentiality. When we briefed the elders, it was with a clear understanding that it was to be with complete confidentiality. However, one of the almost disastrous leaks came through the wife of an elder.

When we needed to assist financially, the elders were forthcoming with the funds. In addition, Rahab and Agnes did get help from charity organisations and contacts linked to Rahab's employer.

The Board of Elders never confronted Pastor Jehu. He never came to church again once the matter became known to us. He tried to get a teaching contract at a local Bible College. When the matter was raised with me and I briefed the office on the situation, they did not hire him. After this, Pastor Jehu went to another part of the country where I am told he got himself another wife. Eventually, he was found guilty, tracked down by the police, arrested, and imprisoned.

In the meantime, Agnes finished high school and got a scholarship to study abroad. She is unlikely to return home soon. One brother has proceeded to university in the United Kingdom. Only the youngest son is home with his mother. Rahab continues to be actively involved in the church. She occasionally briefs me on the children's progress.

While I cannot say with certainty that I handled the matter in the best possible way – only God can judge that – I am convinced that I did what I could. Rahab tends to think so.

Lessons from Rahab

As we look at this example, we notice that those involved did a number of things well.

The school counsellor believed Agnes's disclosure and the Women's Hospital provided good counsel. Rahab, her mother, also did well by believing her daughter. After Agnes reported the rape to Rahab, she immediately arranged for a woman in the church to take Agnes to the hospital. This quick action enabled medical evidence to be established as this is crucial for any prosecution to go forward under the country's laws.

However, despite believing Agnes's story, no one helped Agnes get to safety. It is horrifying to think that after Rahab had medical confirmation that Agnes had been the victim of incest, she allowed her daughter to stay in that situation. She had full knowledge that Agnes would likely be raped again. By assenting to the CCTV, it could be said she was almost encouraging that scenario so that they would be able to prosecute him.

One might say that Rahab was only following the suggestions made by Agnes, since Agnes is the one who suggested installing the CCTV in order to gather evidence. But Agnes was a child who had been traumatized by repeated violence. Protecting her was the responsibility of the adults.

It is impossible to imagine how absolutely terrifying it would be to allow oneself to be raped again – and for the purpose of being filmed in order to show others! This is an unthinkable level of retraumatization for the victim.

What does it say about the level of Agnes's desperation that she would even suggest this? We must also remember that Pastor Jehu had threatened Agnes and her loved ones with death if she told anyone. Agnes had taken a huge and terrifying risk by telling someone. How devastating to finally take that risk and then to hear that there was not enough evidence to sustain a case in court. Did this mean nothing would ever change? She likely reached out for the only option of escape she could think of.

It is shocking that medical evidence of abuse would not be enough to sustain a case in court. Even if that is the case, no further proof was needed for the adults to get Agnes to safety. We must do better if we are to take seriously our call to protect children.

Lessons from John

We turn now to John's response. John did well to be concerned about the reports and to show a willingness to get involved, especially after Agnes's abuse was verified. This included giving information to the pastor who was counselling Pastor Jehu, the lawyer representing him, and the Bible College administration that was considering hiring him as a lecturer. Perpetrators often hide information, which gives those who are seeking to help them the wrong picture. John's action prevented misunderstanding and further harm.

However, we should also look closer at John's initial hesitancy to get involved. He states that he was not an elder, nor part of the church leadership and felt he could not approach the elders without a witness.

It should not be a requirement for the abused person to make a direct report. The victim may be scared that they will be belittled, ignored, dismissed, or retraumatized in the process of making the report. What could John have done? Since the girl did not want to speak on her own, she might have been persuaded to do so with the support of John and his wife. Culturally, difficult matters are often handled through an intermediary because of the age or power differentials between those directly involved.

It seems John felt that he did not have a voice, but is this really true? As we saw earlier, Proverbs 31:8-9 says, "Speak up for those who cannot speak for themselves, for the rights of all who are destitute. Speak up and judge fairly; defend the rights of the poor and needy." For abuse to stop, those who have knowledge or even a concern that abuse may be taking place cannot remain silent. Unfortunately, since no one acted on the first report, Pastor Jehu was given an opportunity to continue his abusive behaviour.

John's feelings that he could not go to the elders without a witness could have also been based on his interpretation of Paul's statement in 1 Timothy 5:19: "Do not entertain an accusation against an elder unless it is brought by two or three witnesses." This instruction was given for the protection of an elder who, because of his position, might be open to attacks from those who would maliciously seek to bring him down or undermine his ministry.

But does that mean that John could not raise a concern until he found other witnesses? Does this mean that an elder could not even hear a concern regarding the conduct of another elder without two or three witnesses? If we take that interpretation, an elder could be involved in much evil and yet never be called to account because there would not be sufficient witnesses for each individual incident. But sexual abuse rarely has witnesses. Therefore, because of the lack of witnesses, Pastor Jehu would never be confronted with his sin.

A better understanding of this text is offered by Albert Barnes when he says that the elder "was not to regard an accusation against a presbyter [elder] as *proved*, if there was but one witness in the case" (emphasis mine).[63] The need for proof is a legal requirement in order to formally accuse someone of a crime, but it is not necessary for someone to report a concern, for the church to look into the report, or even to take precautions to get victims to safety. Thus, the elders could receive an accusation as a concern that would require them to look into the matter to see if there was any truth to what was being alleged. It was thus not John's responsibility to gather witnesses before reporting the concern. In fact, in many cases we find that several individuals are being abused by the same person. If they each report their case, there would be plenty of witnesses and evidence even if there were only one witness in each scenario.

John mentions that biblical rules of correcting those in the wrong also prevented him from acting. This may have been based on a misinterpretation of Matthew 18, which tells someone who has been sinned against to directly confront the person in sin, and then take a witness, and finally to bring the matter to the elders. However, as we explained in earlier, this passage does not apply to sexual abuse.

In reporting the case, John could have followed the instructions of Paul in Ephesians 5:11, "Have nothing to do with the fruitless deeds of darkness, but rather expose them," and, instead of leaving Pastor Jehu at large, gone to the elders to speak up about the risks within the church, even without the young lady's testimony.

This raises the issue of confidentiality, which was a key concern for John. This is indeed valid in many circumstances in daily life. However, there is a standard in professional circles for pastors, counsellors, lawyers, and social workers, that limits confidentiality: if there is, or could be, harm to self or to others, it must be reported. Although confidentiality is important, preventing harm is even more so. And so, because John felt he couldn't go to the elders with both the disclosure of the young woman and the concern of the lady at the camp, Pastor Jehu was able to continue the abuse.

Further, John expresses the valid concern that once the issue of Pastor Jehu's sin was known and disclosed to the elders, the wife of an elder breached confidentiality. This should not have happened. However, the greater issue is that once the arrest had been made, and Pastor Jehu was imprisoned, his actions were now a matter of public record, and the elders should have been transparent and made the matter known to the congregation. Although this would have been difficult for Rahab and Agnes, it would have opened the door for other possible victims, such as the young adult woman, to come forward with their stories. It also would have enabled the church to minister to her and other victims as they dealt with their own trauma. This would have helped Rahab and Agnes move forward after the facts were made public. Of course, the details would be kept to a minimum and the statement to the congregation would require careful and sensitive crafting.

Unfortunately, John related that the Board of Elders never confronted Pastor Jehu. Sadly, as mentioned previously, many churches do not confront or discipline their pastors, and instead leave it to civil authorities to deal with the issue. This is a dereliction of their biblical duty and allows the offender to continue without consequences whether in the local congregation or elsewhere. There may be various reasons for the elders' inaction. However, it must be noted that the church did not have a code of conduct nor child safety policies and procedures that would have provided clear and unbiased guidance to help them deal with the issue.

Thus, we come back to the idea of involvement. As much as we believe that government, social agencies, and non-governmental organizations play an important role in preventing child sexual abuse, much can – and should – be done by the church and individuals at the grassroots level. This is where primary protection and action for change can begin and make an immediate impact. In the following chapters, we look at how we can put into practice policies and procedures that will help us to keep our children safe, as well as dealing with those who commit sexual violence and abuse against our children.

PART IV

Preventing Abuse

11

Talking with Children about Sexual Abuse and Safety

An eight-year-old girl we will call Ruth was in primary school and the only child of her parents. She was referred for psychiatric assessment because she was demonstrating fearfulness, breathlessness, anxiety, nightmares, and did not want to go to school. Her mother became concerned and, in questioning her daughter, was told of sexual abuse by the landlord's 17-year-old son.

When she was questioned by the counsellors Ruth was quiet, perplexed, anxious and, at times, unhappy. Initially, she sat on her mother's lap and clung tightly to her. Gradually, she settled down and as a rapport was developed with the counsellors, she was able to describe in detail how the abuse had taken place in her own home while her mother was working for their landlady.

Ruth was able to talk about her experience because the counsellor provided a safe environment for her. We need to break the silence around sexual abuse. If we are going to be provide safety for our children, we need to provide environments that encourage openness and emotional support for the whole family, including both parents and children.

Create a S.A.F.E. atmosphere

My daughter Emily once said, "Everybody needs a good listening to." That statement has become an iconic saying in our family. But for that saying to become a reality we require a safe setting where whatever is being shared will be heard sympathetically and empathetically. Using the acronym "S.A.F.E.", the following are some ways we can develop this safe and secure atmosphere, beginning in the home with your children.

SPEAK ABOUT ANYTHING

Give children permission and invite them to speak about anything. Assure them that it is okay to express their feelings, fears, problems, and challenges. However, when you make the offer you have to be ready for anything they share, nor can you express shock or dismay. To do so will make them feel unsafe and shut down future communication. This freedom to share their lives and what happens to them is important in providing safety for children. This is because if something happens to them, whether that is bullying, unkindness, or abuse, they will know that they can tell you and you will take their report seriously and not dismiss the issue or belittle them.

This means that parents must be willing to talk to their children about difficult subjects, such as sex, even though it may be culturally taboo and uncomfortable. You must explain to them about safe touching and private parts and how to respond if someone tries to touch them or do something that makes them uncomfortable. Also reassure them that it is safe to talk to you should something like this happen. In this way, if someone tries to touch them inappropriately, they will know that they are free to disclose to you, as a safe adult, what has happened.

ACKNOWLEDGE THE VALIDITY OF THEIR FEELINGS

When we allow children to share their emotions, we need to acknowledge those as valid. Feelings aren't "wrong" – they are simply an acknowledgement of reality. John Powell, in his book, *Why Am I Afraid to Tell You Who I Am?*, says, "Emotions are not moral (good or bad) . . . Feeling frustrated, or being annoyed, or experiencing fears and anger do not make one a good or bad person."[64]

So, if a child says, "I am sad," we shouldn't say, "Don't feel that way." Or if they say, "I am angry!" we shouldn't say, "Don't feel angry." Or if they say, "I am afraid," we shouldn't tell them not to be afraid. Instead, we need to acknowledge the reality of their feelings and emotions, and then take it one step further and probe to find out the "why" and the "what" of their feelings. "Why are you sad? What is making you sad?" Or "Why are you angry?" Ask, "What is making you afraid?" By exploring these emotions, we not only validate what they are feeling, but also help them to discover and then deal with the root causes of these feelings.

One writer states: "Being able to communicate and genuinely trying to understand each other's feelings can be very meaningful: 'The most healing gift you can give to someone in pain is the awareness that you are honestly trying to understand what they are going through, even if you get it wrong.'"[65]

How does this apply to child safety? Let me offer an example. Mary has always liked to go to her uncle's house to visit her cousin Jane on Sunday afternoons. One day her mother asks if she is going to go see her cousin and she says, "No, I don't want to."

Her mother asks, "Why?"

Mary replies, "I am afraid to go to her house."

The mother could respond with, "Don't be afraid. You always have fun there." This, however, would dismiss Mary's feelings. Mary has a reason for her feelings that the mother may not understand. So the mother could ask, "Why are you fearful? What is making you afraid?"

Mary may not want to disclose the reason and say, "I just don't want to go." This hesitancy, along with the change of behaviour is a warning sign.

The mother could say, "Is there any reason?" This would give Mary the opportunity to share why.

If the home is a safe environment in which Mary knows she can speak about anything, with this encouragement she may say, "I don't like it when Uncle George is around. He makes me scared."

The mother could respond with, "Don't say that about Uncle George. He is a good man." But this would invalidate Mary's feelings and cut off the conversation.

Or she could ask, "Why does Uncle George make you scared?" At this point, Mary might be ready to disclose that her uncle has touched her inappropriately.

FACE THE STRUGGLES TOGETHER

It is one thing for a child to be able to speak about anything and for an adult to acknowledge the reality of their feelings, but a safe environment is not fully developed until the child has the assurance that when they share their struggles and problems the adult will be there for them and help them to face whatever they are dealing with. This is most appropriate for parents, but may also apply to close relationships with teachers or leaders.

In the case of Mary and her problem with her uncle, her mother and father need to step in and help her deal with the situation. However, this is not always the case. In my research I have been told about children who shared that they had been abused and were slapped or spanked because they reported what had happened to them. This is because they broke the taboo of speaking about sexual issues and thus violated the cultural value requiring respect for their elders.

For the home to be a safe place, the children need to know that their parents will protect them and help them to face their struggles together. Mary's parents need to intervene by confronting the uncle and by setting up safeguards to protect Mary. This may not be easy, but it is a parental responsibility to ensure that the home is a safe and secure haven for their children.

ENCOURAGE ONGOING CONVERSATIONS

Finally, establishing a pattern of continuing conversations about your child's life and struggles, their joys and pain, their victories and defeats demonstrates ongoing care and interest and can help to engrain safety into your environment. Usually, deeper issues need more time and open sharing as children process what they have experienced. This needs to happen in a place where they feel valued, accepted, and safe. For Mary, depending on the severity of the molestation, she may need to talk about it a number of times. The more severe the trauma she has experienced, the more love, support, patience, and reassurance she – and other children in similar circumstances – will need.

Educate children about safety and boundaries

A practical application of the principles we have outlined here is to develop a child safety plan. The following is a brief outline of how to put this protection in place in various settings such as your family, church, and school.

IN YOUR FAMILY

Parents need to take the lead by opening the discussion about what is considered healthy sexual behaviour and what is abusive sexual behaviour.

Of course, this should be done in an age-appropriate manner. Have this conversation from time to time with all family members – children, teenagers, and adults – in order to establish appropriate and inappropriate sexual behaviour and ensure that they understand and remember the information.

Teach children the proper names for body parts and about "safe touch" and what to do if someone tries to touch them inappropriately. Some abusive behaviour may not involve touching at all; for example, showing pornography to a child is abusive, even if the child is not physically touched in any way. Another issue is the easy availability of internet pornography that children can easily access via computers and cell phones. Parents should discuss this issue openly with their children and use screening apps or programs that restrict access to pornographic sites.

Set clear family guidelines for personal privacy and behaviour. Discuss them with all members of your family and actively model these guidelines personally and with other adults who spend time around or supervise the children (for example, if a child does not want to hug or kiss someone hello or goodbye, they can shake hands instead).

This conversation should not only include teaching about sexual abuse from adults but also inappropriate child-to-child sexual behaviour. This is more common in some cultures than others, but overall, this activity is on the increase. As more children have access to the internet through computers and an increase in smart phone usage, they are able to view pornography more easily. As a result, they may act out what they have seen. Parents can help to provide protection to their children by helping them understand this danger from other children.

If you are concerned about the inappropriate sexual behaviour of a parent, cousin, sibling, other family members, or someone outside the family, care enough to talk to them. If you have developed a S.A.F.E. family atmosphere as outlined above, your family will know that they can talk to you about any inappropriate behaviour that may already have occurred, and that you love them and will work to get them help.[66]

AT CHURCH

You can also address the issue in your church. There is a church in the Nairobi area that teaches all their children in Sunday school, along with their parents, about child safety. This includes instruction about safe touch, "private parts", how to say "no", and the importance of reporting any incident that may be considered unsafe or sexually abusive. One little boy, who was about five years old, came to his father not long after the training and told his father that their house help was touching his private parts. Since both the father and the boy had received the training, they had a common vocabulary and, as a result, the abusive situation was brought to light and immediately dealt with. This illustrates that involving the children along with their family members can have a direct impact on the family.

AT SCHOOL

If you have your own school-age children or work in a school setting, you need to be aware of the possibility of sexual abuse within the school context. Research has shown that pupils can be in danger of abuse from school staff and fellow pupils. Some students walk to school or take public transport and are thus exposed to the possibility of abuse from the public. Boarding schools have their own unique risk factors. Ways to lessen the risk of abuse should be discussed and implemented with the participation of the students.

Schools have a key role to play in protecting children. Every community is different, but it is good practice for teachers to listen to pupils and to understand what the risks to children might be on the way to school. For example, sometimes children take short cuts that are dangerous, particularly if a girl is walking on her own. In Tanzania, teachers beat school children with a stick if they were late for school. This led children to take short cuts to get to school on time or hitch a ride with a truck driver or on a motorbike, thus exposing themselves to the possibility of being abused.

So, the school could tell children it is better to be late and safe and stop punishing occasional lateness. They could advise children to walk in groups, or at least with a friend, because there is generally safety in numbers. They should be helped in considering the routes they take as they walk to school to see whether there are ways that are less isolated. This may mean avoiding certain footpaths or routes even if it means they walk a little further. Students can also be encouraged to vary their routes if possible so that there is no distinguishable pattern that may be picked up on by someone who might want to do them harm.

For those who use public transport, it would also be wise to travel with other students, if possible. Having adults take students to where the public transport picks them up or meet them there on their return, if practicable, also promotes safety.

Additionally, schools must be safe places! "Marks for sex" – when male teachers give good marks in exchange for sex with female pupils – is extremely immoral. Schools should do everything possible to be aware of this and have a zero-tolerance approach to anything that puts pupils at risk. One basic and unbreakable rule should be that no teacher is permitted to be alone in a closed room with a pupil – boy or girl. This is a simple way of creating transparency and avoiding high-risk situations.

12

Preventing Abuse and Providing Protection

I was teaching at a seminar on child safety when one of the pastors got up and told of how one of the children of the church had been sexually abused in the church compound. What was difficult for him was that it happened during the church service and what made matters worse was that it happened in the pastor's own home. It was crushing for him to know that this could have happened right under his nose. He was desperate to know how he could prevent something like this from happening again.

We might wonder, too, how we may prevent abuse from occurring. It would have been helpful if the three underlying principles that promote child safety had been in place. These principles are the foundation upon which a strong child safety policy is built. They are: increased accountability, decreased isolation, and a balance of power. These three points are intertwined and overlap, although there are different practical applications. Let's look at how these would work in the context of children's ministry in the following scenario.

Elizabeth loved teaching the children in her Sunday-school class and looked forward to meeting them every week. Arriving at the church, she went to the pastor's office and greeted him, telling him that she would be in the Sunday-school classroom. In the classroom, she sat down quietly to pray for the children who would arrive soon. Then, behind her, she heard the door open and close unexpectedly and was surprised when she heard the shuffle of feet. Opening her eyes, she saw Benjamin watching her. Smiling, she welcomed him, and walked over to swing the door open wide.

As she stepped outside to see if there was another teacher or any other children around, she noted Benjamin's mother sweeping the church. She greeted her with "Good morning, Mama Benjamin, how are you this morning? I am glad to see that Benjamin has come to Sunday school. Thank you for bringing him to my class today. He is going to help me set up the chairs in the classroom."

Stepping back into the room, she noticed several other children entering the church compound. Smiling, she and Benjamin busily arranged the room so that it would be ready when the rest of the students flocked into the room.

Increase accountability

It is a basic principle that, in providing child safety, church staff should act in a safe, caring, and responsible manner with a high level of accountability. So, in the course of ministry to children, which may involve one-to-one interaction, there are a number of ways to increase accountability. The first way Elizabeth increased accountability was by informing the pastor of her presence and where she would be. By doing this, she was being open about her activity and location. Often cases of abuse happen when no one knows the presence or whereabouts of the perpetrator. As often as possible, let others know where you will be, who you will be with, and the time period the ministry will take place.

There are other ways to increase accountability in ministry situations. If teachers or volunteers are transporting children to an activity, they should notify parents and their ministry leaders. If staff are involved in the counselling of children or dealing with a private issue, inform other staff members and seek to be visible to others in this one-on-one situation. Finally, if in an emergency, staff members must provide transportation and will be alone with a child, they should find another individual to accompany them and, if that is not possible, inform the parents and the ministry supervisor or other church leader of the situation. This will provide an increased level of accountability.

Thus, increasing accountability means that in dealing with children others are aware of what we are doing, where we are, and what the planned activities will be. By being open and transparent about these establishes certain expectations of the nature of our ministry.

Decrease isolation

Decreasing isolation means that individuals who work with children are not left alone with a child and that there is open visibility of teacher-student interaction. This includes leaving classroom doors open and installing windows in doors or classrooms so that anyone can see what is taking place at any time. In this way, one is visible to other adults at all times.

How did Elizabeth decrease isolation? First, she did this by adding visibility to the context. The door did not have a glass windowpane, so Elizabeth opened the door. In this way, anyone passing by could look into the room and see both her and Benjamin. She also looked outside the classroom and, seeing Mama Benjamin, alerted her that she was with Benjamin, thus practically decreasing the isolation factor.

There are other ways to decrease isolation in ministry contacts. One is by putting into practice the "two-person" rule. The Child Safety and Protection Network describes how individuals working with children can avoid isolation as follows:

> At least two adults should be present in group work with children. An adequate number of adults should supervise [children's] events, especially overnight activities. Isolation can easily be overcome by avoiding being alone with one child. For example, take two or more children to the bathroom together, rather than only one; drop off siblings last in a carpool or take your own child along when providing rides, or employ principles of visibility or accountability.[67]

If possible, the two adults should be unrelated, simply because there have been examples of family members protecting each other when abuse has taken place.

Balance of power

Balancing power means recognizing that an adult – by virtue of their age and social status – is able to overpower, control, influence unjustly, or manipulate a child. Therefore, one adult with one child may be equal in terms of numbers of adults to children, but it is not an even distribution of power. In other words, the numbers of adults and students need to be evenly distributed according to *power* rather than numbers in the context of ministry.

The Child Safety and Protection Network describes the principle:

> When working with children balance the age, size, strength, power, and authority between staff and children to help lower risk. This can be done by such things as sending two same age children to the bathroom with an adolescent or adult helper, dropping off siblings last in a carpool, or having a friend play in the room while talking to student after [class or the event], or inviting two or more students to your home to work on a project.[68]

How did Elizabeth work toward establishing a balance of power? Because she had arrived early, she did not expect to be alone with a student. She did not have many options available to her when Benjamin arrived unexpectedly, which is often the case. However, she did look for other adults in the vicinity and when she saw the other students coming, she felt that she could now without difficulty re-enter the room with Benjamin.

As illustrated in this scenario with Elizabeth, we see that we may sometimes find ourselves in situations that are not ideal for child safety. We should not panic, but take reasonable steps and precautions to minimize the risk of being misunderstood and consider what may help us provide safety for the children under our care.

In light of these foundational principles, let's think again of the story of the child abuse in the church compound. First, there seems to be little accountability in place. There was, for instance, no accountability for either the well-being of the child and or the adult taking care of the children. Unfortunately, many churches offer little supervision for their children. They are often left to themselves while the adults attend the worship service. This makes the children vulnerable to abuse. In some cases, there are far too few adults for the number of children present. This increases the possibility that an unsupervised child could wander off alone, and could easily wind up in an isolated situation that makes them vulnerable to abuse.

Secondly, the pastor's house provided an isolated venue for the abuse to take place. There was simply no one else around at the time. Thus, the adult could perpetrate the abuse by isolating the child behind closed doors or in a dark room. Without any form of accountability, it was easy to get the child alone.

Thirdly, there was no balance of power. One adult with one child is an imbalance of power. There should always be at least two unrelated adults with the child or one adult with several children to make sure that the proper balance is maintained.

A policy that incorporates these three foundational principles and is *practised* creates an atmosphere of safety within the church.

13

Recruiting and Hiring Staff

If your church, school, or organization interacts with or serves children, it is very important to consider who you hire or enlist as a volunteer to work with the children. When we recruit staff or volunteers, we need to recognize that anyone could have the potential to abuse children in some way. In addition, sometimes offenders will be transferred or move to another post where people are unaware of their history. Therefore, Christian organizations need to screen prospective pastors, leaders, and those who are working with and ministering to our children so that we do not hire past offenders. There are reasonable steps we can take to ensure unsuitable individuals are prevented from working with children.

In churches, it is common to have more volunteer workers than employees, whereas in NGOs the workers are generally employees with fewer volunteers. Therefore, there will be a primary difference in how the workers in both organizations are handled, both in the hiring and dismissal processes.

While there is overlap in the recruitment process, recruitment in churches is much more informal and often based on the willingness of a member of the church to volunteer their time and involvement. On the other hand, hiring a worker for an NGO often involves a formal recruitment and application process. When there is a concern raised about child abuse by a staff member or a volunteer within the organization, it is a legal issue in both an NGO and a church. The process for an NGO must, however, be more thorough and intense because failure to do due diligence could make the NGO legally liable for any abuse caused by one of its workers.

In an NGO, reports of abuse are also a Human Resources issue. In a church where a volunteer is involved, they are a church discipline issue, but abuse within an NGO can very easily become a church discipline matter as well because employees of a Christian NGO would most likely be members of the church and thus under their spiritual authority as well.

While each church or NGO will have its unique hiring and onboarding procedures, they should include a robust application and screening process. These two work hand in hand to help the organization determine the suitability of applicants for their ministry.

Although often there are pressing personnel or staffing needs, no applicant should ever start their responsibilities in a church or NGO until the entire application and screening process is completed. Allowing individuals to begin ministry or work before they are vetted not only opens the organization to the possibility that harm might be done to children, but also to legal liability.

Application process

First, all staff and volunteers must complete an application form that should include three written references from referees not related to the applicant. These should preferably be from previous employers or pastors, thus removing partiality and personal bias. The application form and written references should be received before prospective staff or volunteers are even interviewed for the position. I have provided a sample application form for children's ministry in a church context at the end of this chapter.

Secondly, all staff and volunteers should undergo a criminal background check. The availability and value of these checks may vary greatly, depending on the local context, but still should take place if possible. Those applicants who are expatriates and come from countries that conduct credible background checks should provide documentation along with their application.

In addition, all staff and volunteers must sign a declaration stating whether or not they have ever had a complaint made about them concerning children. This is especially important if local staff and volunteers come from a context where criminal background checks are not viewed as credible or hold much value. This signed declaration demonstrates that the organization has done the proper due diligence should a lawsuit ever be instituted against them following a case of child abuse in their organization.

An example of a self-disclosure statement on the application would be: "I hereby confirm that I have not previously been convicted for any offence involving any type of harm or sexual abuse to a child or children. To my knowledge, I know of nothing that would affect my suitability to work with children."

Along with this self-disclosure statement, the application should include a truth declaration statement signed by the applicant. A simple example of this statement would be: "I declare and affirm that the information provided in this application and supporting documents is true and correct."

It is important that the self-disclosure statement and truth declaration statement be dated and signed by the applicant as part of their application and kept securely in their file. Although one would not expect an applicant to confirm that they have been convicted of child abuse, nor lie about the information submitted with their application, these two documents remain a legal protection for the organization in that it demonstrates that they have done their due diligence.

Thirdly, in the hiring process all staff should have either a Contract of Employment, or Memorandum of Understanding as well as a clearly defined job description. Additionally, all volunteers should have a volunteer's agreement outlining their duties, time, and supervision arrangements. Both staff and volunteers should also be required to sign the organization's code of conduct. This will enable the organization to take action to dismiss them in the case of misconduct.

The concept of a written code of conduct is alien in many communities, either because literacy levels are not high or writing things down or signing a form denotes mistrust and fear. Forcing people to comply when they don't really understand the reasons can be counterproductive and leads to window dressing – in other words, it looks good but nothing has changed. An NGO or church has the right to expect staff to agree to its code of conduct, but the implementation can be tailored for the culture. The roll out and training around this is very important as well because it gives people a chance to speak, push back and decide on what the values of their organization are and should be. This is, of course, with input from the organization's leadership in terms of what the non-negotiables are and why. So much of how this is done depends on the cultural context and is best delivered by local workers who truly understand child safety and are familiar with the culture.

Screening

Because the organization is involved with children, they must conduct pre-engagement screening of both staff members and volunteers. The screening process starts with the application as described earlier; the second step would then be an in-person interview with the applicant comprising standard questions regarding their qualifications for the position for which they are applying. Interviews are most common for hiring staff or leaders of children's ministries; they may not be necessary for all volunteers in a church context.

In addition, the interview should include specific questions that would help raise possible red flags about the individual's suitability to serve with the NGO. Be sure to ask the applicant about their viewing of pornography. The question should not be framed as, "Have you ever viewed pornography?" but rather, "When was the last time you viewed pornography?" This then gives the interviewer the opportunity to ask follow-up questions about how they have handled their viewing activity and what steps and safeguards they have taken to stop the practice and to be held accountable. This is important because there is a well-understood connection between the use of pornography and child sexual abuse.

The interviewee should also be asked whether they have ever been involved in the molestation, abuse, or mistreatment of children. While one would not expect an applicant who is intent on gaining access to children to admit such action, asking the question protects the NGO by showing they have done due diligence to protect the children in their care. There are a number of other red flags to be aware of. At the end of the chapter you will find a list of red flags that has been compiled for the hiring of teachers and staff in Christian schools. You can refer to this list and adapt it to your own setting.

Another simple step in the screening process is to check the applicant's online and social media presence. Generally, viewing public information posted on social media in the hiring process is not illegal. However, profiles often contain protected class characteristics such as race, religion, age, and gender that in some countries would be illegal to use in determining whether a person is qualified to be hired.[69] It is wise to check your country's laws.

Social media presence may be limited, but it can sometimes show "red flags" that raise some concerns about the applicant's suitability for ministry or in your NGO. A checklist is included at the end of this chapter. Some of the things to look for are provocative or inappropriate photographs, videos, and information, extreme political or religious posts, discriminatory comments related to race, gender, or religion, for instance.[70] This social media check will give you a broader view and understanding of the applicant than may be obtained from the written application and interview. This step can be taken for staff and volunteers.

Evaluating the application and interview information

After the application and interview process has been completed, it is important that those doing the hiring evaluate the information they have received. There are several factors to consider before bringing the applicant onto the staff. First, follow up properly on the references provided. Personal contact with the referee to get a firsthand review of the applicant is the best way to confirm what you have learned from the process about their character, skills, and experience. If there are red flags raised or inconsistencies between what was given by the applicant and from the information obtained from the referee, it is better to look for another individual to fill the position. Red flags should be examined and, if found to be true or likely true, the person should not be hired. In this way, you will be protecting the children you minister to as well as your organization's ability to continue ministry.

The application and screening process does not just entail evaluating the skills, education, and experience of the applicant. As a Christian organization or church, you are also looking for their spiritual maturity and how they may fit in with your organization's values. How will their personality and communication styles contribute to a positive workplace culture? Are they respectful and kind to the people they serve and to fellow workers? Are they honest, humble, and able to resolve conflict well? Do they recognize their need for repentance and God's grace?

It is always easier to appoint another applicant to a position than to get a problematic employee out of it, so carefully evaluate all the information you have gathered from the screening process to make sure you have the right person for the right position.

Of course, applicants can still lie or cover up information. A friend who works in a children's home had to fire staff members for sexual abuse and yet all these employees had had clean criminal background checks, had signed their child protection policies, and had even trained other staff on these policies. However, because the organization had clearly prioritized and communicated the importance of child safety, these staff could not claim ignorance or innocence when they were confronted and the organization could not be held liable for the actions of their staff.

For this reason, even when you have vetted staff, it is still important to maintain good safety practices and take reports of abuse seriously. However, by screening applicants from the beginning you will have taken an important step to safeguard your organization, your staff, and the children with whom you work.

Finally, all appointments should be made conditionally on the successful completion of the probationary period of not less than three months. This will give the leadership or administration time to observe and evaluate the new staff member or volunteer as to their suitability and competence to carry out their responsibilities.

Children's Ministry Application Form

CHURCH NAME:			
CHILDREN'S MINISTRY APPLICATION FORM			
Name:			
Date:			
Phone:			
Email:			
Position Applying for:	Teacher		
	Assistant		
	Other: (Please specify) ____________		
Are you a church member?	Yes:	No:	
What church were you a member of before you came to <CHURCH NAME>?			
What previous experience, if any, have you had in teaching or working with children? Please describe:			

From *Safe! How You Can Protect Children from Sexual Abuse* | © Philip E. Morrison | Published by Oasis International Ltd.

Employment history: What previous employment positions have you held? Please describe:	
Name of employer:	
Phone:	
Postal address:	
Email:	
Name of employer:	
Phone:	
Postal address:	
Email:	
Name of employer:	
Phone:	
Postal address:	
Email:	
References: Preferably of an institutional nature or organizations where the applicant has previously worked with the children instead of personal or family members. One should be from the applicant's former pastor.	
Name:	
Position held by referee:	
Postal address:	
Phone:	
Email:	
Name:	
Position held by referee:	

From *Safe! How You Can Protect Children from Sexual Abuse* | © Philip E. Morrison | Published by Oasis International Ltd.

Postal address	
Phone:	
Email:	
Name:	
Position held by referee:	
Postal address:	
Phone:	
Email:	
Applicant self-disclosure statement: I hereby confirm that I have not previously been convicted for any offence involving any type of harm or sexual abuse to a child or children. To my knowledge, I know of nothing that would affect my suitability to work with children.	
Applicant's signature:	
Date:	

From *Safe! How You Can Protect Children from Sexual Abuse* I © Philip E. Morrison I Published by Oasis International Ltd.

Red Flags*

APPLICATION RED FLAGS

1. Inaccurate information or approximate dates
2. Employment gaps
3. Attention to detail failures
4. Job jumping
5. Backwards movement or plateau
6. Failure to follow directions
7. Unusual employment history
8. They don't declare any information that is likely to appear on a disclosure form (background checks)

CV/RÉSUMÉ RED FLAGS

1. Unprofessional
2. Lack of customization
3. Missing/erroneous information
4. Gaps in employment record
5. No numbers

INTERVIEW RED FLAGS

The interviewee:.

1. Doesn't show up or is late and then doesn't apologize.
2. Is unprepared, unprofessional and impolite
3. Is not willing to admit their flaws or weaknesses
4. Shows a lack of adaptability or willingness to learn
5. Exhibits a high degree of drama and negativity and/or has extreme views
6. Provides inconsistent or vague answers and/or conflicting information
7. Is unable to explain gaps in their employment or doesn't supply information that is likely to appear on a disclosure form

REFERENCE CHECK RED FLAGS

1. Perfectly positive – seems too good to be true
2. Avoids specifics
3. Inconsistency – facts don't match to applicant's CV or résumé
4. Vague answers

From *Safe! How You Can Protect Children from Sexual Abuse* I © Philip E. Morrison I Published by Oasis International Ltd.

* The list of "red flags" was compiled by the TeachBeyond Safeguarding Team of Bronwen Coe, Allison Neumann, and Matt Godfrey. Used by permission.

5. Negative feedback
   - Who are the references from? Check their backgrounds and how long they have known the applicant.
   - Who is the spiritual reference from? Does this person really know the applicant?

BACKGROUND CHECK RED FLAGS

1. Professional licenses
2. Sanctions, disbarment, or disciplinary actions against professional license
3. Reportable criminal convictions
4. Inconsistencies in education
5. Discrepancies in skills
6. Behavioral concerns

SOCIAL MEDIA SCREENING RED FLAGS

1. Provocative or inappropriate photographs, videos, or information
2. Extreme political, religious postings
3. Evidence of excessive drinking and drug use
4. Discriminatory comments related to race, gender, religion, etc.
5. Bad-mouthing previous employers or fellow employees
6. Unprofessional screen name (e.g. hotbabygurl@hotmail.co.uk)
7. Confidential information being shared
8. Inappropriate language

SAFEGUARDING INTERVIEW RED FLAGS

1. Only wants to work with children because they fulfill an emotional need.
2. Has no instincts or knowledge of safeguarding principles.
3. Has no self-soothing techniques/emotional maturity.
4. Has no sense of professional boundaries.
5. Answers "yes" to any of our three specific questions:
   - Has there ever been a concern raised or a complaint made against you regarding your conduct, whether related to safeguarding or any other matter?
   - Have you ever received a caution, reprimand, or warning, or been convicted of a criminal offence or investigated by any statutory authority?
   - Is there anything past or present that might hinder your interaction with children, young people, and vulnerable adults (depending on workplace laws), such as medical issues, emotional/mental health, addictive behavior (pornography, drug use, alcoholism)?

From *Safe! How You Can Protect Children from Sexual Abuse* | © Philip E. Morrison | Published by Oasis International Ltd.

14

Policies

We must exercise duty of care on behalf of children under our care and within our organizations and ministries. This means that we put measures in place to prevent child abuse and protect children from harm. It is essential that your church, school, or NGO has a child safety policy that outlines how the organization operates in order to protect children. It is an administrative safeguard against harm and abuse to children that protects staff and volunteers in the course of their ministry. It should consist of the organization's specific child-protection protocols, including guidelines for reporting concerns of abuse, steps for preventing abuse, requirements for training, a specific code of conduct, and human resource procedures if a staff member has acted inappropriately.

Perhaps a chapter on policies seems dry or technical. Perhaps procedures seem like unnecessary paperwork or rules. But all organizations already have policies in place: about how many days of leave employees are allowed to take, and how to deposit or withdraw money from the church or organization's bank account. If these matters are important enough for us to create a policy, surely protecting our children is important enough to be something that we clearly explain and enforce in our churches and organizations.

The value of policies and procedures

I want to point out the value of policies and procedures. First, policies and procedures are *educational*. As you begin to share a policy with church leadership and those who work with children, various issues of child safety will naturally come up and an established policy thus becomes a tool for training and educating those responsible for children's ministry in the church. I worked with a church in Nairobi to put its policy in place and they planned to have all the church elders and leaders, along with the Sunday-school teachers, take the training based on this policy.

Secondly, policies and procedures are *protective*. This is why we put them in place to start with. I came across this announcement in a church bulletin: "We make an appeal for more volunteers to join . . . the Sunday-school (teachers and helpers)." I have heard similar announcements made during a church service. However, these churches had no policy when it came to the screening of those who might come to serve. Without a screening policy in place, it is more difficult to protect our children from volunteers who might harm them. Such a policy will help protect our children, child workers and the church itself. This is why they are so essential.

Thirdly, policies and procedures *give guidance*. Church leadership may be concerned about child safety, but not know how to go about it or know what to do if a child in their congregation is abused. But having a policy to follow will give them an unbiased path to follow. This is especially important if a church leader or member is involved in the abuse. The church can take action based on the policy rather than on the personality.

Fourthly, policies and procedures are often *required*. Many NGOs depend on their status as a charity in order to receive funding from outside sources. Many of these donors now require NGOs to have a child safety or child protection policy. Governments are also starting to require this for faith communities.

The Republic of Kenya's "County Child Protection Systems Guideline" makes this statement:

> Organisations providing services to children shall prove their commitment to upholding child protection standards by developing child protection policies . . . All staff, whether in direct or indirect contact with children . . . shall sign a statement of commitment to child protection as part of their employment contracts. These shall include police officers, teachers, doctors and nurses, all other state and non-state actors (NGOs, CBOs, faith communities) coming into contact with children in the line of their duty.[71]

In Tanzania, UNICEF worked closely with the government to research violence against children and create a "National Plan of Action to Prevent and Respond to Violence against Children", involving the various sectors of the police, justice system, health and social welfare services, HIV/AIDS sector, education, religious groups, and civil society.[72]

It is likely that many other countries have – or will have – similar laws requiring any organizations that work with children, including churches, to have written child safety policies guiding their interaction with children. So, for the safety of our children, and compliance with the regulations that are coming, let me encourage all of us, in our denominations and in our local churches, to put in place policies and procedures as soon as possible.

The world is beginning to take sexual violence against women and children seriously. But in my research I found very little to indicate that the church is doing much about this. When we are slow to respond on this issue, we let the world – and sometimes ungodly people – shape the argument and decide how society should respond. Then the church ends up disagreeing and opposing their approach instead of proactively helping to shape the argument and response from a biblical perspective. As God's people, let's take the lead on issues of child safety.

Customize your policy

After the conclusion, a sample policy is given for a church context. This policy is contextualized for Africa, but may need to be adapted for a local church's unique context and setting. It is highly probable that there will be differences between urban and rural churches that may require further adjustments to the basic policy.

There are helpful online tools that provide a starting point for other organizations. For instance, the Child Safety and Protection Network (https://cspn.org) provides resources for missions and Christian schools in developing child safety policies and protocols for safeguarding within an organization.

Because policies are required, you may be tempted to simply download or "cut and paste" a policy from another organization just to tick a box.

Doing this means your organization is less likely to understand, embrace, or contextualize the policy. I encourage anybody who has a policy or is writing a policy to make it relevant to their context and align it with the core values of the organization. A contextualized and relevant child safety policy will be one that grows out of the vision of your organization and demonstrates how child safety fits integrally with it.

Any adaptations and adjustments should still retain and maintain the basic principles of increasing accountability, decreasing isolation, and balancing power that are foundational for a policy to provide safety for the children of the church.

While there are many aspects to a policy, special attention should be given to the central importance of an organization's code of conduct as it outlines the standards expected of hired staff. It forms part of the terms and conditions of employment. Some organizations will have a separate code of conduct that relates specifically to volunteers, consultants, and contractors and will form part of their contract with the organization.

Periodic training

Creating a policy is the first step, but you must also *implement* the policy. It is important to ensure that all your staff, as well as any volunteers who work with children, know and follow the policy. Your NGO or church should have regular child safety training for all paid and volunteer staff. It is recommended that training be done on a yearly basis. The value of yearly training is that it keeps the importance of child safety and protection at the forefront, and elevates the issue as a priority within the organization. This is especially true where there is a high turnover among staff and volunteers.

In conjunction with this training, the code of conduct should be periodically signed by all paid and volunteer staff even if they have signed it before and then kept on file in the human resources or church office. It is recommended that this signing be done at least every two years.

Yearly training also means that as new staff members are hired or new volunteers join, although they are required to sign the organization's code of conduct, they will be brought up to the same level of existing staff. In this way, they will be able to have the same understanding of the organization's child protection vocabulary and reporting procedures if they become aware that child abuse has taken place.

Leadership

Without leaders behind an initiative and supporting its implementation even the best programmes or projects will fail. Therefore, if your organization or church decides to put into place child safety policies and procedures these must be supported by the top administrators. Leaders must be in the forefront of encouraging child safety within the organization and actively participating in the required training and signing of the organization's code of conduct.

Attorney Samantha Kilpatrick who advises faith-based organizations on abuse prevention says,

> As a pastor and church leader, I urge you to be proactive in creating, reviewing, and enforcing policies, educate your staff and volunteers to be vigilant and to follow policies, get out in your community and find resources that will help you on this journey, and when you do receive a report of abuse, utilize those community contacts.[73]

Similarly, Rachel Denhollander, a survivor, attorney, and advocate for victims of abuse, writes to church leaders: "You must take the lead in pursuing the truth and show by your words and conduct that it's what you really want . . ."[74]

At a child safety training event of a large NGO, they played a video message from their international director who shared his appreciation for what they were doing and emphasized his full support of the importance of child protection within their ministry. This type of support from an organization's highest leadership urges other members to comply with the policy and procedures that have been put in place.

Another aspect of leadership that is needed is that the organization should provide as a permanent position a child safety officer. Depending on the size of the organization, this position does not necessarily need to be a full-time one. In a smaller organization, it can be a responsibility given to another employee along with other duties. This is important in order to ensure that regular training is held as well as having a person who can handle reports of abuse that may arise within the organization.

Without someone keeping this concern in the forefront of the organization's practice it can easily be ignored or forgotten. One organization I know of had written policies and procedures in place, but did not follow through on them. When one of their members was involved with child sexual abuse, it was discovered that the person's supervisor was not aware of their organization's policies and procedures. It seems that no particular individual was specifically responsible for maintaining and promoting child safety and thus children under their care were abused. If safeguarding were indeed an important part of their organizational culture, they would have followed the policies and procedures written into their administrative documents.

We have a duty to protect our staff members, volunteers, and the children under our care. We can avoid repeating the sad situations described earlier if everyone – from the leadership down to the volunteers – prioritizes child safety and protection.

15

You Can Change the Story

A man came up to me before the morning church service. His wife had been abused by her father and we had spoken about her journey towards healing. I could tell he was upset because he didn't even greet me, but blurted out, "I have just discovered another case of incest."

I put my hand on his shoulder and replied, "I am so sorry."

He rushed on, "If it is this bad here [meaning the church], what is it like out there?" I shook my head in agreement. Then he said, "What you are doing is so important."

As I write this closing chapter, let me thank you for reading this book, because that indicates that you feel that protecting children within your church or NGO is very important. Before we can begin to impact the world "out there" we must first begin to impact our churches and organizations. It will only get better "out there" when it begins to be better "in here." It will only get better when we begin to change the story of child abuse in our churches and NGOs.

I have dedicated the last 10 years of my life to seeking to protect children and responding to situations of abuse in an effort to bring justice, hope, and healing into the lives of those who have been abused and harmed. I have joined others who have the same passion and calling. But, as we have seen in this book, the evil is overwhelming, and the challenge is huge. We need more people to be engaged in our righteous cause. The psalmist asks, "Who will rise up for me against the wicked? Who will take a stand for me against evildoers?" (Psalm 94:16). Our children are asking the same thing. We need you to respond with, "I will."

In Scripture we have examples of those who rose up against the wicked and stood in the gap, acting and interceding for God's people to keep them safe in times of crisis.

- Moses, in a time of national idolatry in the golden calf incident at Mount Sinai (Exodus 32).
- Phineas, in a time of national immorality when the Israelites were seduced into sensual Baal worship (Numbers 25).
- Aaron, in a time of national insubordination (Numbers 16).

And now we live in a day and age when the sin of child sexual abuse is an indescribably and incomprehensibly evil and vile attack aimed at the most vulnerable members of our society. We cannot stand idly by. We can change the story of the vast number of children who are now or in danger of being abused. To change their story, we must stand in the gap for them in the midst of our present-day moral crisis and advocate for their safety.

How can you stand in the gap? How can you change their story? What you have read in this book gives you the tools to start making a difference in your church or NGO and even beyond, in your community. Let me offer a few suggestions.

Begin with yourself. Some readers may already be familiar with child safety principles and procedures, but perhaps you have learned some new ways of protecting children. I encourage you to add them to your practices of child protection. Some of you have begun to educate yourself simply by reading this book. I urge you to continue reading and learning about protecting children. There are always new dangers that emerge – through technology, social media, changing attitudes, and culture. Learn about your local and national government's child protection laws. Discover which organizations in your community provide child protection services.

Secondly, begin in your own home, teaching your family the basic child safety principles such as safe touch and saying, "No!" to unwanted interactions. This can start in early childhood with age-appropriate language and examples. Encourage your children to be aware of their environment and to observe the foundational practices of visibility, accountability, and the balance of power. Help them to know how to respond in situations when someone makes advances or seeks to harm them.

Thirdly, be a champion for child safety in your church and the schools your children attend. Perhaps your pastor or the headmaster of your school has not even considered the issue of child sexual abuse or the need to develop and put into practice protective policies and procedures. You can make a difference by sharing what you have learned from this book in advocating for the children who attend the church or school. As part of this effort, educate and enlist other parents and community members to make these places safe and free from abuse.

If you are working in an NGO, you can do the same for your organization. Does your NGO have a child protection policy and proper procedures in place? If it does not, volunteer to head up a committee to develop these. If there is already a policy in place, determine whether it is being followed. Is the NGO's staff being trained in the policy's procedures? This is especially important if the NGO has a ministry or provides services to children. Do a facility audit to determine whether there are actions that can be taken to improve visibility in offices and places where children are being cared for. Talk to your leadership team and offer to help train the staff and volunteers.

As you have read this book, my hope is that God is giving you a vision of how you can be used by him to protect children. However, vision alone will not accomplish the reality of providing safety for our children. One of my favourite quotes comes from Walter Isaacson, who wrote a biography of Leonardo da Vinci. He said, "Vision without execution is hallucination."[75] Vision must be achieved through intentional and proactive action. It will be accomplished when you and many others stand in the gap for our children and help keep them safe!

A Sample Policy Template

Church Child Sexual Abuse Protection Policy

<CHURCH NAME> seeks to provide a safe and secure environment for the children who participate in our programmes and activities. By implementing the practices outlined below, our goal is to protect the children of our church from incidents of misconduct or inappropriate behaviour while also protecting our staff and volunteers (workers) from false accusations.

From *Safe! How You Can Protect Children from Sexual Abuse* | © Philip E. Morrison | Published by Oasis International Ltd.

1. DEFINITIONS

1.1. Definition of a child. According to The Children Act, 2001 the Kenyan government defines a child as "any human being under the age of eighteen years."[76]

1.2. Definition of child sexual abuse. "Child sexual abuse ... is 'the involvement of a child in sexual activity that he or she does not fully comprehend, is unable to give informed consent to, or for which the child is not developmentally prepared and cannot give consent, or that violates the laws or social taboos of society.' Child sexual abuse is evidenced by this activity between a child and an adult or another child who by age or development is in a relationship of responsibility, trust or power, the activity being intended to gratify or satisfy the needs of the other person. This may include but is not limited to: the inducement or coercion of a child to engage in any unlawful sexual activity; the exploitative use of a child in prostitution or other unlawful sexual practices; the exploitative use of children in pornographic performance and materials."[77]

1.3. Definition of Worker. The term "worker" would include anyone involved in a church ministry (Sunday School, Vacation Bible School, church camps, etc.), a church-sponsored school, overnight activities involving minors, counselling of minors, or one-on-one mentoring of minors.

2. WORKERS

2.1. Requirements and screening

All persons who desire to work with the children participating in our programmes and activities will be screened. This screening includes the following:

2.1.1. Requirements

- **Teachers:**
  - A teacher must be a member as defined by the local church.
  - A teacher must be a person who is born again and evidencing Christian growth and maturity.

  - A teacher must regularly attend worship services and other church events and not only be involved in the children's ministry functions.
- **Assistants:**
  - A non-member, as defined by the local church, may be an assistant worker.
  - An assistant worker must be a person who is born again and evidencing Christian growth and maturity.
  - An assistant worker must regularly attend worship services and other church events and not only be involved in the children's ministry functions.
- **The Six-month Rule.** No person will be considered for any ministry position involving contact with minors until she/he has been involved with <CHURCH NAME> for a minimum of six (6) months. This is a time of prequalification that provides opportunity for interaction between our leadership and the applicant, allowing for better evaluation and suitability of the applicant for working with children.
- **Age Requirement.** All teachers must be at least 18 years of age.
- **Probationary Period.** All new teachers and assistants (both adult and teenage) will go through a probationary period of four months under the supervision of an approved teacher.

2.1.2. Screening

Written Application. All persons seeking to work with children must complete and sign a written application in a form to be supplied by us (see Children's Ministry Application Form). The application will request basic information from the applicant and will inquire into previous experience with children, if any, previous church affiliation, references and employment information.

All applicants shall sign a self-disclosure form confirming they have not previously been convicted for any offence involving any type of harm to a child or children and declare anything that may affect their suitability to work with children.

2.1.3. Reference Checks

Before an applicant is interviewed for work with children, at least two of the applicants' references will be checked. These references should be of an institutional nature as opposed to personal or family references, preferably from organizations where the applicant has worked with children in the past. One should be from the applicant's former pastor. Documentation of the reference checks will be maintained in confidence on file at <CHURCH NAME>.

2.1.4. Personal Interview

Upon completion of the application, a face-to-face interview may be scheduled with the applicant to discuss his/her suitability for the position.

From *Safe! How You Can Protect Children from Sexual Abuse* | © Philip E. Morrison | Published by Oasis International Ltd.

2.1.5. Confidentiality

All application documents will be maintained in confidence on file at the <CHURCH NAME>.

2.2. Teenage workers

There may be times when it is necessary or desirable for child ministry workers who are themselves under age 18 to assist in caring for children during programmes or activities. The following guidelines apply to teenage class-assistant workers:

- Must be at least age 14.
- Must be screened as specified above.
- Must be under the supervision of an adult and must never be left alone with children.

From *Safe! How You Can Protect Children from Sexual Abuse* I © Philip E. Morrison I Published by Oasis International Ltd.

3. ADULT OVERSIGHT GUIDELINES

3.1. The two-adult rule

It is our goal that a minimum of two unrelated adult workers will be in attendance at all times when children are being supervised during our programmes and activities. Some youth classes may have only one adult teacher in attendance during the class session; in these instances, doors to the classroom should remain open and there should be no fewer than three students with the adult teacher. We do not allow minors to be alone with one adult on our premises or in any sponsored activity unless in a counselling situation.

3.2. Mixed male-female groups

Where there are mixed male-female groups there must be male and female leaders. In case where, for example, there is a girls' group with a male facilitator/leader, there must also be a female facilitator/leader present.

3.3. Visible ministry policies

- No workers are ever to be alone with a child. At least two workers should be present whenever possible.
- If a child arrives early, keep the door open and remain visible.
- Doors without a glass pane installed should never be closed completely when children are inside with adults.
- When holding a private talk with a student, especially of the opposite sex, be sure to sit in view of an open door or window.

3.4. Toilet facilities

- <CHURCH NAME> will seek, as possible, to provide or reserve separate toilet facilities for males and females. As much as possible, separate facilities will be provided for boys and girls.
- For children under five years of age, workers should escort a group of children to the toilet. They should always be taken in a group, never

a child alone. Workers should check the toilet first to make sure that it is vacant, and then allow the children inside. Workers should remain outside and then escort the children back to the classroom. If a child is taking longer than seems necessary, the worker should call the child to check whether assistance is needed.

- For the protection of all, workers should *never* be alone with a child in a toilet with the door closed. If a child requires assistance, the workers should always leave the door open far enough that other workers can see in. Do not allow the children to "watch" while another child is using the toilet.
- For children over the age of five, at least one adult male should take boys to the toilet and at least one adult female should take girls. The worker should check the toilet first to make sure that the toilet is vacant, and then allow the children inside. The worker should then remain outside the toilet door and escort the children back to the classroom.
- Parents are strongly encouraged to have their children visit the toilet before class.

4. CODE OF CONDUCT[78]

Workers involved in children's ministry agree not to:

- Engage in inappropriately rough physical play with a child or young person (excluding their own).
- Use physical means or corporal punishment to discipline or control a child, other than reasonable restraint such as by holding a child to minimize injury.
- Hold, kiss, cuddle, or touch a child (excluding their own) in an age/culturally inappropriate manner OR in a manner considered inappropriate by reason of the nature of the programme/activity/occasion/event, except for appropriate touch (to comfort distress, for example).

5. RESPONDING TO ALLEGATIONS OF CHILD SEXUAL ABUSE

If a worker involved in the care of children at <CHURCH NAME> becomes aware of suspected sexual abuse of a child under his/her care, this should be reported immediately to the <NAME OF PERSON TO WHOM ABUSE SHOULD BE REPORTED> for further action, including reporting to authorities as may be mandated by state law. This verbal report should be accompanied by a written Abuse Incident Report. (See Abuse Incident Report.)

From *Safe! How You Can Protect Children from Sexual Abuse* I © Philip E. Morrison I Published by Oasis International Ltd.

If an incident of child sexual abuse is alleged to have occurred at <CHURCH NAME> or during our sponsored programmes or activities, the following procedure shall be followed:

5.1. The parent or guardian of the child will be notified.

5.2 The worker or church member alleged to be the perpetrator of the abuse must immediately cease involvement in ministry pending an investigation and instructed to remain away from the premises during the investigation. He or she should be instructed to have no contact with either the victim or witnesses.

5.3. <CHURCH NAME> commits to report allegations of abuse to the civil authorities and to fully cooperate with their investigation of the incident.

5.4. <CHURCH NAME> must designate a spokesperson to the media concerning incidents of abuse or neglect. The advice of legal counsel will be sought before responding to media inquiries or releasing information about the situation to the congregation. All other representatives of <CHURCH NAME> should refrain from speaking to the media.

5.5. A pastoral visit will be arranged for those families who desire it. This should be for the purpose of providing pastoral support during the time of crisis and not for the purpose of investigating the incident or influencing the investigation.

5.6. Any person found guilty of the alleged abuse or misconduct must be removed from their position working with children or youth. At this point the perpetrator will be turned over to the governing authorities so that the legal process may take its course.

6. RESPONDING TO THE NEEDS OF THE VICTIMS OF CHILD SEXUAL ABUSE

<CHURCH NAME> commits to the following pastoral care ministry for the family and victims of child sexual abuse who experienced the abuse while involved in an official ministry of the church:

6.1. Providing a medical examination and treatment for the victim.

6.2. Pastoral and professional counselling for the victim and his or her family.

6.3. Legal counsel and advice for the victim and the family.

6.4. Financial support for the above pastoral care ministries.

From *Safe! How You Can Protect Children from Sexual Abuse* | © Philip E. Morrison | Published by Oasis International Ltd.

7. TRAINING

<CHURCH NAME> will provide training on this child protection policy to the following:

7.1. All church leaders. They will go through training on this policy and its requirements regardless of whether they are involved in children's ministry or not.

7.2. All new childcare workers. In addition, <CHURCH NAME> will strive to provide opportunities for additional training classes or events on an annual basis. All workers are strongly encouraged to attend these training events.

7.3. All parents of children who attend any of the various children's ministries of the church.

7.4. All children who attend the various children's ministries of the church. Training will be done in an age-appropriate and culturally sensitive manner.

From *Safe! How You Can Protect Children from Sexual Abuse* | © Philip E. Morrison | Published by Oasis International Ltd.

To download a free customizable version of this template and other resources from this book in various languages, scan this code or go to **oasisinternationalpublishing.com/book/safe/**

Endnotes

1 This story is adapted from Njeri Rugene, "Kenya's children under siege as cases of sexual abuse soar," *Daily Nation,* June 10, 2019, https://www.nation.co.ke/lifestyle/dn2/Sexual-abuse--Why-have-we-betrayed-our-children-/957860-5151838-fbpr8z/index.html, accessed December 3, 2019

2 In my research I found that reported statistics on child sexual abuse worldwide are at similar levels. We look specifically at statistics of child sexual abuse in the church later.

3 Denis McCrann, "An Exploratory Study of Child Sexual Abuse in Tanzania," 10-11, https://arrow.tudublin.ie/cgi/viewcontent.cgi?article=1080&context=appadoc, accessed November 2, 2018.

4 Executive summary to United Nations Children's Fund Kenya Country Office, Division of Violence Prevention, National Center for Injury Prevention and Control, U.S. Centers for Disease Control and Prevention, and the Kenya National Bureau of Statistics, *Violence Against Children in Kenya: Findings from a 2010 National Survey. Summary Report on the Prevalence of Sexual Violence Against Children in Kenya: Findings from a 2010 National Survey. Summary Report on the Prevalence of Sexual, Physical and Emotional Violence, Context of Sexual Violence, and Health and Behavioral Consequences of Violence Experienced in Childhood*, 14, Nairobi, Kenya, 2012, https://resourcecentre.savethechildren.net/pdf/vac_in_kenya.pdf/, accessed June 25, 2016.

5 The age considerations used to define child sexual abuse are 18 years of age and under. Statistics from 2013 tell us that the total population of Kenya (2013) is 43,178,100, and 48.69 per cent of the populace are under the age of 18 years (approx. 21,023,417): UNICEF, "Kenya Statistics", https://www.unicef.org/infobycountry/kenya_statistics.html, accessed November 29, 2016.

The median age was 18.93 years. "Kenya – Age – Median age of the total population," https://knoema.com/atlas/Kenya/topics/Demographics/Age/Median-age-of-population, accessed November 26, 2016.

Violence Against Children in Kenya: Findings from a 2010 National Survey found that levels of violence prior to age 18, as reported by 18- to 24-year olds . . . indicate that during childhood, 32% of females and 18% of males experience sexual violence." If we assume that the population under 18 was similar in 2010 and 2013, and we assume 50% of those under 18 are male and 50% female, we can make a rough approximation that the real numbers of children suffering from child sexual abuse would be 3,363,747 girls and 1,892,108 boys for a total of 5,255,855.

6 Ministry of Labour and Social Protection of Kenya, Department of Children's Services. "Violence against Children in Kenya: Findings from a National Survey, 2019." Nairobi, Kenya: 2019, 31, https://www.unicef.org/kenya/media/1516/file/2019%20Violence%20Against%20Children%20Survey%20(VACS)%20.pdf, accessed September 15, 2023.

7 International Child Advocacy Network, http://www.yesican.org/definitions/who.html, accessed July 16, 2016.

8 Beth Swagman, *Preventing Child Abuse* (Grand Rapids, Michigan: Faith Alive Christian Resources, 2003), 5.

9 Private email, August 1, 2018, used by permission by the author.

10 Philip E. Morrison, "The Study of Child Sexual Abuse Safety Protection Procedures and Interventions in Selected Churches of the Africa Inland Church-Kenya" (DMin. diss. Africa International University, 2018), 145-146.

11 Andy Baker, ed., Gender Equality and Sexual Exploitation (Oxford, United Kingdom: Oxfam Publishing, 2006), 162.

12 Ibid., 163.

13 Maggie Black, *The African Report on Violence Against Children* (Addis Ababa: The African Child Policy Forum, 2014), 47.

14 Report of the Independent Investigation: The Southern Baptist Convention Executive Committee's Response to Sexual Abuse Allegations and an Audit of the Procedures and Actions of the Credentials Committee, May 15, 2022, by Guidepost Solutions LLC, https://static1.squarespace.com/static/6108172d83d55d3c9db4dd67/t/628a9326312a4216a3c0679d/1653248810253/Guidepost+Solutions+Independent+Investigation+Report.pdf, accessed August 23, 2023.

15 Joe Carter, "The FAQs: Report Reveals Sexual Abuse Cover-Up by Southern Baptist Entity," May 23, 2022, https://www.thegospelcoalition.org/article/faqs-sexual-abuse-southern-baptist/, accessed August 23, 2023.

16 African Union, *African Charter on the Rights and Welfare of the Child*, Preamble, https://au.int/sites/default/files/documents/30913-doc-acrwc-en.pdf, accessed November 8, 2023.

17 African Union, *African Charter on the Rights and Welfare of the Child,* Article 11, Section 5, https://au.int/sites/default/files/treaties/36804-treaty-african_charter_on_rights_welfare_of_the_child.pdf, accessed September 22, 2023.

18 Thoko Kaime, *The African Charter on the Rights and Welfare of the Child: A socio-legal perspective* (Pretoria: Pretoria University Law Press, 2009), 39-40,

https://www.pulp.up.ac.za/monographs/the-african-charter-on-the-rights-and-welfare-of-the-child-a-socio-legal-perspective, accessed November 17, 2015.

19 "Minutes, Task Group on Sexual Abuse of Children," 12 March 2020, "Sexual Abuse of Children: public hearings," https://pmg.org.za/committee-meeting/1246/, 12 March 2002, accessed December 22, 2015.

20 Linda M. Richter quoted in Cynthia Grant Bowman and Elizabeth Brundige, "Child Sex Abuse within the Family in Sub-Saharan Africa: Challenges and Change in Current Legal and Mental Health Responses," *Cornell International Law Journal* 47, No. 2 (Spring 2014), 250, http://scholarship.law.cornell.edu/cgi/viewcontent.cgi?article=1841&context=cilj, accessed December 23, 2015.

21 Hassan O. Kaya quoted in Kempe Ronald Hope Sr., ed., *AIDS and Development in Africa: A Social Science Perspective* (London: The Haworth Press, 1999), 42.

22 The Tanzania Ministry of Community Development, Gender and Children, *Child Development Policy,* Second Edition, 2018, 22-23, http://www.cdftz.org/files/Child%20Development%20Policy-2008%20English%20Version%202010%20 (2).pdf, accessed November 5, 2018.

23 Kaime, *The African Charter,* 106.

24 ACPF, *The African Report on Violence Against Children* (Addis Ababa: The African Child Policy Forum, 2014), 44, https://app.box.com/s/iclv9c70sigmceyl30ym, accessed December 17, 2015.

25 ACPF, *The African Report on Children with Disabilities: Promising Starts and Persisting Challenges* (Addis Ababa: The African Child Policy Forum 2014), 36, https://www.africanchildforum.org/index.php/en/sobipro?sid=175, accessed December 19, 2015.

26 ACPF, *The African Report on Violence Against Children*, 52.

27 Charles Ohene-Amoh, "The Uniqueness of the African Charter on the Rights and Welfare of the Child," 12, https://www.academia.edu/10017380/The_Uniqueness_of_the_African%20Charter%20on%20the%20Rights_%20and%20Welfare%20of%20the%20Child, accessed December 17, 2015.

28 Marcia J. Bunge in *Who Is Jesus Christ for Us Today?,* Andreas Schuele and Günter Thomas, eds. (Louisville, Kentucky: Westminster John Knox Press, 2009), 171.

29 Diane Severance, "Jesus Loved Children," May 3, 2010, Christianity.com, https://www.christianity.com/church/church-history/timeline/1-300/jesus-loved-children-11629553.html, accessed May 28, 2018.

30 Ibid.

31 Ibid.

32 Hilda Bih Muluh, *The Girl with Special Shoes* (Chicago, Illinois: Oasis International, 2023), 19-21.

33 Kaime, *The African Charter,* 106.

34 Jennifer Greenberg, *Not Forsaken* (Charlotte, North Carolina: The Good Book Company, 2019), 129.

35 Leslie Vernick in *Becoming a Church that Cares Well for the Abused,* Brad Hambrick, ed. (Nashville, Tennessee: B&H Publishing Group, 2019), 19-20.

36 Jamie Ivey, "Walking with the Broken," *Light* 6, No. 2 (2020): 43, The Ethics & Religious Liberty Commission.

37 Ministry of Labour and Social Protection of Kenya, Department of Children's Services. "Violence against Children in Kenya: Findings from a National Survey, 2019." Nairobi, Kenya: 2019, 31, https://www.unicef.org/kenya/media/1516/file/2019%20Violence%20Against%20Children%20Survey%20(VACS)%20.pdf, accessed September 12, 2023.

38 Wendy Maltz, *The Sexual Healing Journey: A Guide for Survivors of Sexual Abuse* (New York: HarperCollins Publishers, 1992), 4.

39 Diane Mandt Langberg, *Counseling Survivors of Sexual Abuse* (Xulon Press, 2003), 194.

40 Samantha Kilpatrick in Hambrick, *Becoming a Church that Cares Well for the Abused,* 68.

41 Jan Morrison, *A Safe Place* (Colorado Springs, Colorado: Waterbrook Press, 2002), 142.

42 Ali Dorey, Ian K. Duffield, Julie Upton, "Rediscovering Lament as a Practice of the Church – Especially on Deprived Housing Estates," https://theologyandministry.webspace.durham.ac.uk/wp-content/uploads/sites/303/2022/09/TheologyandMinistry1_8.pdf, accessed August 21, 2018.

43 Adapted from "Parts of a Lament," by Dr Gisela Roth from her "Trauma Healing" Workshop.

44 Mike Edmondson, in Hambrick, *Becoming a Church that Cares Well for the Abused*, 166.

45 Boz Tchividjian, "'If your brother sins against you' . . . and he's a sex offender," Arts & Culture, November 14, 2014, https://religionnews.com/2014/11/14/brother-sins/, accessed July 12, 2019.

46 McCrann, "An Exploratory Study of Child Sexual Abuse in Tanzania," 233.

47 Phyllis Kilbourn and Marjorie McDermid, eds., *Sexually Exploited Children: Working to Protect and Heal* (Monrovia, California: MARC Publications, 1998), 194.

48 Victoria L. Johnson, *Children and Sexual Abuse* (Downers Grove, Illinois: InterVarsity Press, 2007), 24.

49 Walter Brueggemann, *Living Toward a Vision* (Philadelphia: United Church Press, 1982), 107.

50 Sources for this story include: Lindsey Blest Van Ness, "Woman's effort in international child sex abuse case helps land former Lancaster County man in jail," February 4, 2021, https://lancasteronline.com/news/local/womans-effort-in-international-child-sex-abuse-case-helps-land-former-lancaster-county-man-in/article_b0e7dcae-66fb-11eb-a7ea-233e6566d345.html, accessed December 13, 2022.

51 William D. Reyburn, *A Handbook on The Book of Job* (New York: United Bible Societies, 1992), 530.

52 New Scent Centre International, http://newscentcentreintl.org/, accessed September 6, 2022.

53 *Life Application Study Bible, New Living Translation, Second Edition* (Carol Stream, Illinois: Tyndale House Publishers, Inc. 2007), 393.

54 Van Ness, "Woman's effort in international child sex abuse case."

55 James Newton Poling in *Telling the Truth: Preaching about Domestic and Sexual Violence*, John S. McClure and Nancy J. Ramsay, eds (Cleveland, Ohio: United Church Press, 1998), 80.

56 Greenberg, *Not Forsaken*, 194-196.

57 Ibid, 184.

58 Ibid.

59 Miroslav Volf, *Exclusion and Embrace* (Nashville, Tennessee: Abingdon Press, 1996), 138.

60 James W. Fowler as quoted in Millard J. Erickson, *Christian Theology, Second Edition* (Grand Rapids, Michigan: Baker Books, 2002), 609.

61 I use the masculine pronoun here and elsewhere simply because the vast majority of perpetrators are male. However, the fact is that there are female perpetrators as well.

62 This account was related to the author in a private email conversation.

63 Bible Hub, "1 Timothy 5:19: Barnes' Notes on the Bible, https://biblehub.com/commentaries/1_timothy/5-19.htm, accessed September 5, 2022.

64 John Powell, *Why Am I Afraid to Tell You Who I Am?* (London: Fount Paperbacks, 1999), 40.

65 Department of Veteran Affairs, "Session Five-Communication Tips for Family Members," 88, https://www.ouhsc.edu/safeprogram/05Communication.pdf, accessed December 2, 2019.

66 This outline has been adapted. See Joan Tabachnick, "Tip Sheet: Create A Family Safety Plan", https://www.stopitnow.org/ohc-content/tip-sheet-create-a-family-safety-plan#, accessed December 10, 2019.

67 McCrann, "An Exploratory Study of Child Sexual Abuse in Tanzania," 233.

68 Ibid.

69 Amber Potier, "The Use of Social Media in Recruitment and Selection: Risk vs. Reward," Appalachian State IOHRM Program, https://iohrm.appstate.edu/alumni/professional-development-articles/use-social-media-recruitment-and-selection-risk-vs-reward, accessed March 2, 2023.

70 Jonathan A. Segal, "Legal Trends: Social Media Use in Hiring – Assessing the Risks, https://www.shrm.org/hr-today/news/hr-magazine/Pages/0914-social-media-hiring.aspx, accessed March 2, 2023.

71 Republic of Kenya, "County Child Protection Systems Guidelines," 213.3, https://bettercarenetwork.org/sites/default/files/County-Child-Protection-Guidelines-2013.pdf, pages 19-20, accessed September 28, 2023.

72 United Republic of Tanzania, "Multi Sector National Plan of Action to Prevent and Respond to Violence Against Children: July 2013-June 2016," https://files.mutualcdn.com/tfg/assets/files/2013-National-Plan-of-Action-to-Prevent-and-Respond-to-Violence-against-Children-in-Tanzania.pdf, accessed September 22, 2023.

73 Samantha Kilpatrick, in Hambrick, *Becoming a Church that Cares Well for the Abused*, 177.

74 Rachel Denhollander, in Ibid., 157.

75 Walter Isaacson, *Leonardo Da Vinci* (New York: Simon & Schuster, 2017), 4.

76 The Children Act, 2001, 11.

77 World Health Organization, 2003, "Guidelines."

78 Adapted from *Staff and Volunteer Pledge*, www.safeplaceservices.org.au, accessed January 23, 2017.

THE MULTI-CHURCH PASTOR

Philip E. Morrison

For pastors who would like to learn how to solve the unique and complex issues of leading more than one congregation, *The Multi-Church Pastor* gives step-by-step guidance.

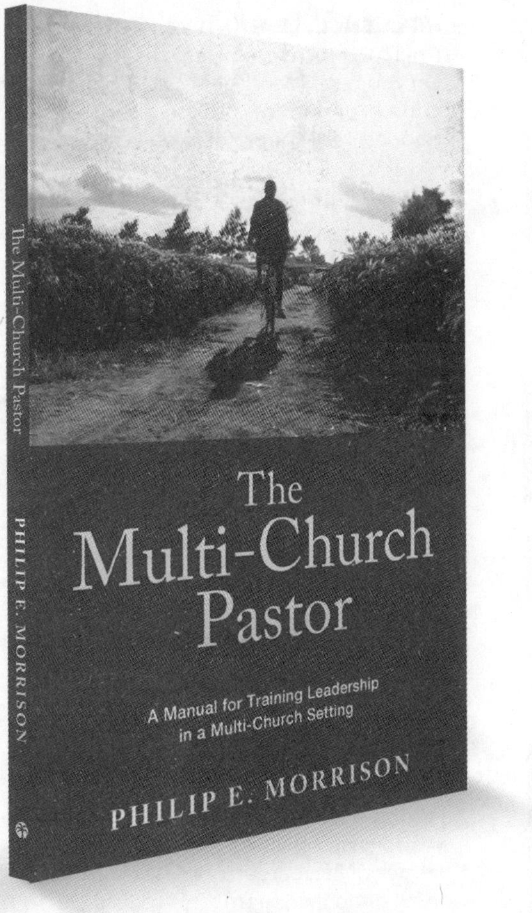

Pastors can learn how to raise up the elders in their churches to lead with them. The skills they learn from *The Multi-Church Pastor* can be applied by pastors whether or not they have formal ministerial training.

OASIS INTERNATIONAL PUBLISHING

oasisinternationalpublishing.com | oasisinternational.com

More Books By Philip E. Morrison

Philip E. Morrison moved to Kenya 25 years ago. As a lecturer at Moffat Bible College, he became passionate about equipping under-resourced pastors who are responsible for multiple congregations.

As a result, he founded The Multi-Church Pastor Institute to mentor and train these pastors. In addition to *The Multi-Church Pastor*, he is the author of:

INFLUENCE: LEADING WITHOUT POSITION
Philip E. Morrison & Hankuri Tawus Gaya
Do you have ideas for how to change your community, church, or nation – but feel powerless to make them happen? This book tells you how you can influence others to take action and start change, just as young men and women in the Bible did.

CONFLICT RESOLUTION IN THE CHURCH
Philip E. Morrison with Chris Mwalw'a
This book is an answer to the great need the church has for a practical approach to conflict resolution in the church. It focuses on scripturally-based, peace-making attitudes within the African church context.

FALLING ASLEEP IN THE LAP OF DELILAH
Philip E. Morrison
Falling Asleep in the Lap of Delilah is a treasure trove of wisdom on finishing the race of life well. Facing the final stages of life, career, or ministry can be daunting and instil deep fear. Morrison's thoughtful insights and powerful mediations on the life of Samson can guide you in preserving your relationship with God and with others.

OASIS
INTERNATIONAL
PUBLISHING

oasisinternationalpublishing.com | oasisinternational.com

AFRICA STUDY BIBLE, NLT

God's Word Through African Eyes

The *Africa Study Bible* is the most ethnically-diverse, single-volume, biblical resource to date. Written by 350 contributors from 50 countries, it includes the Holy Bible: New Living Translation, and more than 2,600 features that illuminate the truth of Scripture with a unique, African perspective.

The *Africa Study Bible* is a monumental study Bible, with notes by scholars and pastors in Africa who see the critical need to make Scripture relevant to our everyday lives. It's an all-in-one course in biblical content, theology, history, and culture.

"The Africa Study Bible *is a model of contextualized engagement of the Scriptures, with notes written by Africans, written for Africans, and answers Bible questions asked in African cultural contexts. It's a great encouragement to me to see such a resource available and I recommend it widely!"*

- Dr Ed Stetzer, Executive Director of the BILLY GRAHAM CENTER

Discover more at ***africastudybible.com***

DOWNLOAD THE
***AFRICA STUDY BIBLE* APP**

The Africa Study Bible app is now on the Tecarta Bible App, the world's best study Bible app which is available to download on Google Play Store and Apple App Store.

Download on the App Store

GET IT ON Google Play

Resources for Pastors

There are many resources which can equip your leading and ministry, including some which have been created in Africa for our contexts. Oasis recommends:

THE DISCIPLER'S TOOLKIT
George M. Mutuku and Mark A. Olander
The churches in Sub-Saharan Africa are growing numerically, primarily through evangelism. But this is only the beginning of the disciple making process. This book takes people from evangelism to establishing new believers in the faith, equipping them in spiritual disciplines and gifts, and sending them out to engage the world with the gospel.

ESSENTIAL LEADERSHIP LESSONS
Richard J. Gehman
Essential Leadership Lessons covers topics of lleadership essentials, humility, love, holiness, attributes, management skills, and common issues. While the context and application of these leadership lessons were created with the people of Africa in mind, the principles of Christian leadership are the same everywhere, for everyone, on all continents.

THE ESSENTIAL GUIDE TO THE BIBLE AND CHRISTIANITY
John Jusu
Situating each book in the context of the whole Bible clarifies truths that are less clear when taken out of context. This guide will help you understand, from a biblical perspective, how the visible world connects with the realities of the unseen world surrounding us.

STAND UP FOR THE GOSPEL
Emmanuel Kwasi Amoafo
This book is a timely wake-up call about what is happening in many of our churches today. It will equip you to defend our timeless faith. In the midst of counterfeits, rediscover the refreshing truths of God's Word, and the glorious, life-transforming gospel of Jesus Christ.

SOLVING CORRUPTION IN THE CHURCH AND NATION
Richard J. Gehman
A major problem is that in practice the Christian church so often reflects the same moral rot found in society. The church has failed to be salt and light. *Solving Corruption in the Church and Nation* shines light on this problem and explores a biblical solution. This book is for you because it points to the solution for this ongoing and unending moral mess.

AFRICAN CHRISTIAN THEOLOGY REVISITED
Richard J. Gehman
For all African Christians, African Christian Theology Revisited is a powerful plea to think through your faith in African contexts under the authority of the Word of God.

AFRICANS AND AFRICA IN THE BIBLE
Tim Welch
This book shows the presence and the participation of Africans in the biblical text, helping demonstrate that Christianity is not a "white man's religion" and that Christianity has deep roots in African soil.

LEARNING TO LEAD
Richard J. Gehman
With its discussion questions and practical applications, this book will guide you to obtaining character and skills and help you become an effective Christian leader. It was written from the living experience of African leaders and it has been shaped by 36 years of training church leaders in Kenya.

BIBLICAL CHRISTIANITY IN MODERN AFRICA
Wilbur O'Donovan
The church in Africa is consumed with conflict, denominationalism, and division. Marriages and families are in great need of family life teaching based on the Bible rather than culture. *Biblical Christianity in Modern Africa* addresses these and more issues and offers suggestions on how these problems can be overcome.

HELPING WITHOUT HURTING IN AFRICA
Jonny Kabiswa Kyazze and Anthony Sytsma with Brian Fikkert
This book trains leaders to proclaim the gospel in both word and deed, changing mind-sets and helping them apply biblical principles to care wisely and compassionately for people who are poor without unintentionally doing harm.

OASIS
INTERNATIONAL
PUBLISHING

Our mission is to grow discipleship through publishing African voices.

Go to oasisinternationalpublishing.com to learn more.

THE SISTERHOOD SECRET
Levina Mulandi
In this book, Dr Mulandi shows how discipling is more than Bible study or a church program. She shares how she empowers any woman to mentor younger women, guiding them to understand their identity, discern the purpose of their lives, and be transformed to be more like Christ.

HAPPILY WHENEVER AFTER
Bookie Adekanye
Candid and kind, Bookie Adekanye reminds you of God's overwhelming love for you. No matter how society labels you, God says you belong to him. You're invited to heal from past scars and be your confident, courageous self. The God of the Bible used single ladies to deliver and save, and he definitely has a plan for you.

BAESICS
Ernest Wamboye with Waturi Wamboye
In Baesics, Ernest and Waturi Wamboye give no-nonsense advice on how to build a fulfilling love life and marriage. Young adults in African cities feel marriage is priority but are often unprepared. Baesics addresses the relationship dilemmas many young adults are facing today from a Christian point of view.

GETTING MARRIED?
Chao Tsuma Wanje and James Wanje
Written as a friendly and light-hearted conversation, this book is perfect for you and your fiancé(e) to read and discuss together. Drawing from timeless wisdom and real-life examples, this husband-and-wife team helps couples to resolve conflicts before they explode.

THE DIVORCE DILEMMA
Ron Misiko & Ray Motsi
The authors share their experiences as pastors and as married people, as well as their areas of expertise in the legal system and Bible scholarship. From their different African contexts, they explain how to navigate the challenges we face today with biblical and practical solutions for divorce care in African churches.

I ONCE WAS DEAD
Cedric Kanana with Benjamin Fischer
This book's riveting, action-packed plot, has one central message shining through: Jesus is stronger than death, than addiction, than Islam, than traditional religion, than curses. Trust Jesus alone! The miracles recorded in I Once Was Dead echo the book of Acts and give all glory to God – whether healing, deliverance, resurrection, protection from threats, or hearing God's voice.

THE GIRL WITH SPECIAL SHOES
Hilda Bih Muluh
Hilda's family didn't know she had muscular dystrophy. They just knew their preschooler was losing her ability to walk. But they were determined to find a cure. *The Girl with Special Shoes* is the witty and heartfelt story of a family's sacrificial love and a God who refashions pain into purpose.

A PRE-MARRIAGE COUNSELLING HANDBOOK
Alan & Donna Goerz
This handbook was written specifically for the African context on how to build a successful marriage. Designed as a seminar-in-a-book, *A Pre-Marriage Counselling Handbook* equips pastors and counselors to teach biblical pre-marriage classes and seminars.

ANSWERS FOR YOUR MARRIAGE
Bruce and Carol Britten
Offers practical insights to marriage issues and facts on sex, pregnancy, family planning, child-raising, money issues, adultery, HIV, and sex-related diseases. If your marriage is in despair, look to this book for some answers for your marriage.

HIGHLY FAVOURED: OUR POWERFUL GOD'S COVENANT WITH YOU
Stuart J. Foster
The God of the Bible is not unreliable or inaccessible like the spiritual beings in African traditional religions. He chooses to have a covenant relationship with his people and we do not have to earn God's favour.

oasisinternationalpublishing.com | oasisinternational.com

SATISFYING AFRICA'S THIRST FOR GOD'S WORD

OASIS INTERNATIONAL
is devoted to growing discipleship
through publishing African voices.

Engaging Africa's most influential,
most relevant, and best communicators for the sake of the gospel.

Creating contextual content that meets the specific needs of Africa, has the power to transform individuals and societies, and gives the church in Africa a global voice.

Cultivating local and global partnerships in order to publish and distribute high-quality books and Bibles.

Visit **oasisinternational.com** to learn more about our vision, for Africa to equip its own leaders to impact the global church.

OASIS INTERNATIONAL
oasisinternational.com

OASIS INTERNATIONAL PUBLISHING
oasisinternationalpublishing.com

GOD'S WORD FOR AFRICA
godswordforafrica.com